Libertarianism in a Nutshell

By Aaron Barksdale & Joshua
Hardy

LIBERTARIANISM IN A NUTSHELL

BROKEN PRESS PUBLICATIONS

Published by Broken Press Publications, LLC

P.O. Box 661, Hurley, MS 39555

This book is an original publication of Broken Press Publications, LLC

First Printing May 2016

For more information about Broken Press Publications, visit
http://www.broken.press

Dedicated to:

My family: Jessica, Skylor, and Aubrie

You are the reason I get up in the morning.

~Aaron

To my wife Sandra for tolerating another crazy idea, and to my children; Christopher, Alexander, and Sarah. It's my plan that you realize that opportunities are not handed to you, they are created.

~Josh

LIBERTARIANISM IN A NUTSHELL

Table of Contents

Introduction

Forward

Libertarianism is many things to many people. To some, it is a philosophy of life. To others, it is a political philosophy. To other people like yours truly, it is both. I often tell people that I would be a libertarian even if no government ever existed in the history of mankind. I would be libertarian in every facet of life. I would be libertarian in my business dealings, in my dealings with other people, and in my dealings with society. But let's not fool ourselves. Government exists. I know it does as I have seen it firsthand. So, as a libertarian, it is incumbent upon me to make sure that the government I live under is restricted in its ability to do harm.

So what is libertarianism? Barksdale and Hardy attempt to answer this by applying libertarian logic to the issues of the day. How would a libertarian solve the healthcare issue, the abortion issue, or the situation in the Middle East? To understand libertarian solutions, you must first understand libertarianism. As I said in the beginning, it is many things to many people. It may be many things to many people, but all libertarians agree on the basic principle of, *it is immoral to use force to impose your will onto another person*. Libertarians express this in many ways. Some call it the Non-Aggression Principle and others simply refer to it as the Absence of Force or Fraud.

To find out if you yourself are a libertarian, simply ask yourself the following questions. Were you born into the involuntary servitude of a majority vote? Can other people simply outnumber you and impose their will onto you? Can they gang up on you and take your money, or gang up on you and force you into their service? We teach our children that when one group of people gang up on an individual and use force to place them into their service, it is known as slavery. But wait, …what if they have a title like Senator or President? What if the vote is 536 to 1? Does this change the nature of the servitude?

The libertarian believes that all human action is only right and just if it involves the mutual consent of the parties involved. For example, during commerce, the buyer and seller can reach a mutually agreeable contract. If the buyer and seller are able to come to a mutually agreeable contract, then it is a good contract. It is actually immoral for outsiders to the contract to get involved and make demands. These "outsiders" can be a majority vote, the Department of Health, or even OSHA. The libertarian believes that the two parties involved in the contract are the only ones that should be involved in setting the terms of the contract. This idea of mutual consent of the parties involved, should apply to all human action. To suggest otherwise, is to suggest involuntary servitude to others.

Many people will use a consequentialist argument to rationalize this servitude. They will tell you that because of the Income Tax, Government is able to provide food for the hungry and medicine for the elderly. They claim because of workplace safety required by OSHA, workplace accidents are reduced. I reject those consequentialist arguments on moral grounds. The Income Tax is nothing more than the Government saying "I have a gun, give me your money". It is the majority ganging up on you and using force to take your money. Where they spend the stolen money is irrelevant. You cannot rationalize theft by claiming that you used the stolen money to buy a hungry person a sandwich, or used it to buy an elderly person medicine. Theft is theft and you cannot rationalize it to a libertarian using a consequentialist argument. The ends do not justify the means.

Danny Bedwell
Former Chairman of the Libertarian Party of Mississippi

Acknowledgments

It took us a minute to think of who really helped us with this book. At first we thought about all the detractors and Statists we argue with and make the same points over and over and over and over again, ad nauseum, but make absolutely no headway. Did they help? In a way, we honed our debating skills; we committed to memory the same points and counter-points to their myriad of questions. We even learned how to bait them into questions that will make a regular statist do something they didn't think they were capable of: think for themselves.

But there is one person who really did help us. He brought me into Libertarianism in the first place, but with his guidance over the years, I wouldn't know what I know now (and without his support, I wouldn't have wanted the State Chair position). Whether it was explaining the nuances of impost and excise taxation or just being an ear to vent to, this person has been there for me my entire Libertarian journey. He has always been accessible and never cross. As chairman, he has supported me in every way and privately coached me when I did something I shouldn't have.

Words cannot express how much I appreciate everything that you have done for me, for Joshua, for the Libertarian movement both in our great state and the nation as a whole. You were there, sitting across from me offering me a choice - two pills: a blue and a red one. If I chose the blue pill, I would wake up, continue supporting the government like a good, little neocon should. However if I took the red one I would wake up to the lie of the two party system and venture into Libertarian Land and see how far down the rabbit hole it goes.

I am grateful for your insight, your guidance, but most importantly, your friendship. Thank you, Danny Bedwell.

Without the help, the input, the insight, and the proofreading (lots and lots of proofreading) from both Joshua and myself, as well as from our family, this book would not be possible. While it's not 300 pages filled with every solution to every problem, it's meant to merely educate on the fundamentals of the principles of libertarians.

So, to all that helped...thanks you.

Preface by Aaron Barksdale

This book is to serve as an educational tool for a better understanding of the principles of Liberty and Libertarianism. This book does not seek to answer all the questions, but merely present an ideology that we hope will educate and enlighten you to see that more freedom for all individuals does not rely on the taking from others of their property, their labor, or their freedoms.

Our country was founded upon the belief that liberty, above all things, was precious. The individual was important, revered. But this will not be a book about how we should "return to a world of our founder's" but rather an understanding of what they were trying to instill in the citizenry. And for several decades, the rights of man were protected and the government was not involved unless someone was physically harmed or their property was harmed.

As Chairman of the Libertarian Party of Mississippi, I owe my transformation from Neo-Con Republican to full-fledged Libertarian to former Chairman of Mississippi, Danny Bedwell. Where many Libertarians I met were akin to the "Paul-bots" that were screaming down anyone that didn't agree with Ron Paul's ideology. My view of Libertarians was groups of shaggy-haired, pot-smoking, anti-war hippies, and that view is shared by many people, on both sides of the political aisle. However, that could not be farther from the truth.

As Danny educated me on the principles of liberty, I began researching some of the people mentioned in the libertarian blogs that I began reading. Reading individuals like Murray Rothbard, Lysander Spooner, and even Frederic Bastiat, along with Danny Bedwell's patient, and often lengthy discussions, that my conversion was nearing completion. That's been almost four years ago, and since jumping into the Libertarian Pool, I have not regretted anything...except why I didn't do this sooner.

Aaron Barksdale

Chairman
Libertarian Party of Mississippi

Preface by Joshua Hardy

My involvement in the political scene began as a devout republican voter. It was no question that every Republican on the ballot was getting my vote. This devotion became watered down during the 2004 presidential campaign. During a speech George W. Bush informed the crowd that if he was reelected, he would do something about the emerging threat of homosexual marriages. At that time only a couple of states recognized homosexual marriages. I realized that if Bush really cared about the issue, he would not wait until reelection to introduce legislation. I began to see that a political game was being played.

During the 2008 Presidential race, I realized that there was absolutely no significant difference between John McCain and Barack Obama. This led me to start my path away from the Republican Party to the Libertarian Party. A friend pointed me to The Mises Institute where I came across several books discussing libertarian philosophy.

During the 2012 election I watched Glenn Beck, Rush Limbaugh, and Sean Hannity flee from Ron Paul and a liberty-based platform because it did not line up with modern conservatism; that is nothing more than conserving the socialist policies that the Democratic Party establishes. If this is not accurate, tell me why Ronald Reagan has more in common with Franklin D Roosevelt and Lyndon B Johnson than he does Thomas Jefferson and Thomas Paine.

After joining the Libertarian Party of Mississippi I decided to run for State House. I was one of a few Libertarian candidates on the ballot and we all received double-digit election results. We have been noticed in this state due to that election cycle. As a result of that election cycle we are in the position to advance liberty in this state. It is my goal that this book helps introduce libertarian philosophy to you as well as pointing you in the right direction to understand more about this subject.

Joshua Hardy

Secretary

Libertarian Party of Mississippi

Infographic: Government Services by Ideology

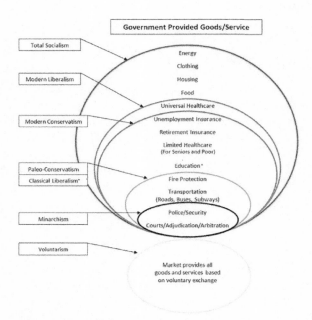

*Some Classical Liberals supported government funded education (ie. Thomas Jefferson), others did not (ie. Bastiat).

https://universityofcommonsense.org

World's Smallest Political Quiz

Before embarking into this book, it's wise to know where you are in your own ideology. This quiz is by far one of the quickest and most accurate tests regarding political ideology.

For each of these questions, you will answer each with the following: (A)gree, (M)aybe, (D)isagree.

Social Issues

1. Government should not censor speech, press, media, or internet.
A   M   D
2. Military service should be voluntary. There should be no draft.
A   M   D
3. There should be no laws regarding sex for consenting adults.
A   M   D
4. Repeal laws prohibiting adult possession and use of drugs.
A   M   D
5. There should be no National ID card.   A   M   D

Economic Issues

1. End "corporate welfare." No government handouts to business.
A   M   D
2. End government barriers to international free trade.   A   M   D
3. Let people control their own retirement; privatize Social Security.   A   M   D

4. Replace government welfare with private charity.   A
    M   D
5. Cut taxes and government spending by 50% or more.   A
    M   D

Each (A) counts 10 points, every (M) counts 5 points, and (D) counts for nothing. To score, total up your SOCIAL Issues score and find that on the left side of the chart. Then starting from there, total up the ECONOMIC issues and beginning where you stopped on the social score, move to the right, in a straight line to find where you fall.

PART I

The Libertarian Coat of Many Colors

Anarchists

The Anarchist is one that does not want a civil government. Anarchy and anarchists have been given a bad name due to those who believe that the State is the only way to have a civilized society. This is the furthest thing from the truth. Liberty minded anarchists believe in an all-volunteer society with absolutely no coercion. This is also known as the non-aggression principle.

As anarchist Emma Goldman stated, "Anarchism stands for a social order based on the free grouping of individuals…" This free grouping can only happen when people respect the sovereignty and freedom of the individual. This means that no person or groups of persons have any dominion whatsoever over another person. This is the natural state of man.

To claim dominion over another person is to show unjust aggression. One cannot be a liberty-minded anarchists and demonstrate unjust aggression toward another. This non-aggression principle is one that makes its way through the entire spectrum of libertarians. If one does not hold to this principle, then the person is not a libertarian.

In this all-volunteer society, people can freely group

together to form whatever type of society that they would like to have. If someone does not believe that this type of system can work, this is not justification for showing aggression toward the anarchists.

The anarchists hold the most pure liberty-minded philosophy of all of the libertarians. They often do not vote because the State always wins in an election. They realize that because the discussion of whether or not the position should be kept is not on the ballot, there is not a possible outcome that is in their best interest. The anarchist is the foundation of libertarian philosophy.

Anarcho-Capitalists

Anarcho-capitalists (or AnCap, for short) are people who believe in a world of Atlantis and John Galt from Ayn Rand's *Atlas Shrugged*. A voluntary society whereby interactions with free individuals can take place, free from government interactions. The main difference between AnCaps and true Anarchists is that Anarchists believe that even a Capitalist market wields authority over individuals and therefore is inherently evil.

AnCaps believe in self-ownership, or moral autonomy. Ask yourself, is your life your own moral purpose? Do you agree that you owe obedience to no one, except by consent? Do you have rights - moral claims to your freedom of action? If you answered "yes" to any of these questions, then logic leads you to the position of philosophical anarchism. According to Robert Paul Wolff (In Defense of Anarchism):

> The defining mark of the state is authority, the
> right to rule. The primary obligation of man is
> autonomy; the refusal to be ruled. It would seem,
> then, that there can be no resolution of the conflict
> between autonomy of the individual and the
> putative authority of the state. Insofar as a man
> fulfills his obligation to make himself the author of

his decisions, he will resist the state's claim to have authority over him. That is to say, he will deny that he has a duty to obey the laws of this state *simply because they are laws*. In that sense, it would seem that anarchism is the only political doctrine consistent with the virtue of autonomy.

If one is a student of history, it is perfectly clear that with all the war, the genocides, slavery and repression that has been perpetrated on individuals has been supported and even practiced by the State. Could humanity be better off without the barbaric institution of "the State?" When you consider that in the 20th Century alone, over 170 MILLION CIVILIANS were killed directly by the State, and many more from the deaths of soldiers, refugees, and so on. Murray Rothbard (father of "anarcho-capitalism" or "Market anarchism") said, "If we look at the black record of mass murder, exploitation, and tyranny levied on society by government over the ages, we need to be loath to abandon the Leviathan State and...try freedom." Let's take a look at some intricacies.

So, you believe in an anarcho-capitalist utopia?

AnCaps tend to be pragmatic. They argue that no matter how good or bad a man is, he is better off in liberty.

If a man is good, he needs no rulers. If men are bad, then governments of men - composed of men - will also be bad, moreover they would probably be worse, due to the State's amplification of coercive power. Most AnCaps understand that not all men are good and that crime will continue to occur. AnCaps do not expect massive change in human nature in that regard. Utopianism, by definition requires a change in human nature, AnCaps do not seek utopia.

Imagine the Utopia from the book and movie version of "The Giver", even that government couldn't alter human nature by default, they had to require daily dosing of their populace in order to CONTROL them. Control the thoughts and you control the thinker.

Wouldn't an anarcho-capitalist, or laissez-faire capitalist society still exploit people?

Laissez-faire literally means "let us be." It means that there would be NO government intervention in the economy. Ideally, a true free market. To understand more of how the government intervenes in the economy, let's go back to Murray Rothbard (from The Myth of Efficient Government Service):

> The vital command posts invariably owned
> monopolistically by the state are: (1) police and
> military protection; (2) judicial protection; (3)

monopoly of the mint (and monopoly of defining money); (4) rivers and coastal seas; (5) urban streets and highways, and land generally (unused land, in addition to the power of eminent domain); and (6) the post office. The defence function is one reserved most jealously by the State. It is vital to the State's existence, for on its monopoly of force depends the ability to exact taxes from citizens. If citizens were permitted privately owned courts and armies, then they would possess the means to defend themselves against invasive acts by the government as well as by private individuals.

Who will build the roads?

One of the most commonly uttered phrases when discussing libertarian, specifically AnCap, philosophy is "Who will build the roads?" Well, let's break that down to specifics. Who CURRENTLY builds the roads? When you speak on the act of BUILDING the roads, this process is usually done by contractors specializing in road construction. These contractors are hired by the municipality, and they are usually the lowest bid...so remember that point.

So, the municipality pays the contractor...but where does the municipality get the money? The taxpayers. The municipality must first TAKE the money from taxpayers in order to pay the contractors. An AnCap would look at this and say, "Why can't we cut out the middleman?"

"Are you talking about private roads?"

Well...yes. In the beginning of the construction of roads, they were all privately built. Factories, farmers, and other businesses built roads in order to get their products from where they were made to the market. In many rural areas these roads still exist as main routes that have been upgraded and are still called "Farm-to-Market Roads" and are maintained by State or local governments. Private roads were the first roads that ran this country.

"But Private roads are toll roads"

Actually, all toll roads in operation today, are owned by a municipality or state. So the argument against private roads because they'll be toll roads doesn't hold water because there are no private toll roads in America. In fact, in Biloxi, Mississippi, a casino approached the City of Biloxi about repairing the road in front of their casino. The City told them that it would be too costly because they would have to do more than just in front of the casino. So, the casino asked if they could pay a company to improve the road. After much consideration, the City of Biloxi agreed to allow the casino to repair the quarter-mile directly in front of their business.

They didn't just repair the road, they improved the street signs, the lights, and the traffic signals. The casino didn't ask for any tolls, nor is there a sign saying "Road Repaired by the Casino". The improvement to the road improved the outward appearance of the casino, which subconsciously, draws people into the casino. After Katrina, another casino did the same.

Without government, who will keep and uphold the law?

First, you have to understand that the "Law" is enforced by the State. And while there isn't a state in an AnCap America, that doesn't mean that there aren't agreed upon terms. First and foremost, all citizens will live according to the simple principles of "Don't hurt people and don't take other people's stuff." Any violations would be subject to a real jury of peers.

Before we dive deeper, understand that the original usage of the word "police" was a verb. And it was the duty of all adult males in a community to do their part, in rotation, of policing their neighborhood to ensure that no individual is harming another or another's property.

In the event that a grievance occurs, the two parties secure a representative (similar to a lawyer) and then the two agree on a judge advocate, one who volunteers or agrees to an amount to be split by both parties. The representatives argue the case based on the best information given to the judge. In issues larger than a few people can decide, or by request of one or both parties, a jury may be convened. All of this happens voluntarily, and not by force of law. Once the matter is settled, all parties return to their respective homes and professions. In an AnCap system, the method of arbitration, as well as who the arbiter(s) shall be, is pre-established, with both parties agreeing to the method of arbitration in the contract.

AnCaps view the free market as a guiding light in the darkness. We will get to the difference between free market capitalism and corporatism, but AnCaps look to the free market for guidance. If you have read *Atlas Shrugged* or watched the movie (primarily Part 3), you will remember John Galt and his utopia, Atlantis. This is an example of the real free market. A collective of individuals producing that which they produce and selling it freely to another based simply upon mutually agreed terms. No government interaction needed.

What about war? Are AnCaps anti-war?

Put into the proper contextual understanding that "war" is essentially violent conflicts between States, then absolutely AnCaps are anti-war. It is probably best understood that

AnCaps do not view global politics in the same statist perspective, but rather as a collection of competing States. AnCaps understand that the rulers of the State and the subjects of those rulers often have very different interests. In war, the Rulers seek to gain power, prestige, and popularity; but the subjects pay the costs in lives, in money, and in standard of living and quality of life. It is best to view war as disputes between petulant power-hungry megalomaniacs.

However, if individuals were enabled to cobble together a band of people to protect their properties collectively for a common goal, like to stop an oppressive government, then you see precisely what happened during a period of time we refer to as the American Revolutionary war. So, many of these quotes are from people you may not have ever heard of, but what about George Washington? In Washington's farewell address, much of what he says are very anti-State. Regarding military he said, "Over grown military establishments are under any form of government inauspicious to liberty, and are to be regarded as particularly hostile to republican liberty."

Okay, I get the anti-war stance, but if you aren't supposed to hurt people, what if someone is trying to hurt you?

Being anti-war or adhering to a non-aggression axiom

doesn't mean you are inherently a pacifist. It merely says that you will not INITIATE aggression. AnCaps are generally pro-gun, pro-self defence. The Castle Doctrine is a very AnCap idea, that man is ruler of his property and has an obligation to protect all who are in and on his property.

The right to protect oneself and property is instinctual. We have already discussed the fact that AnCaps are pragmatic and do not intend to change human nature, why then would AnCaps seek to control your right to protect yourself, or anything for that matter? They wouldn't, it's as simple as that.

While many people struggle with the thought of a voluntary society that is completely devoid of government and governance, many people do believe in certain principles that anarcho-capitalists believe. Some things do not need to have the government involved with, period. If I want to sell my old belongings on my property, the government does not have the inherent authority to shut my yard sale down because I don't have a vendor's permit or require me to pay taxes on the resale of items. Remember, the government only has the authority it has because the people accept the authority and the State.

Minarchist

Minimum-Government Anarchists, or minarchist, is a branch of libertarianism that supports a minimal government, dedicated to preserving individual liberties. In this type of society, there would be heavily restricted government power, minimum spending, and minimal levels of intervention. Minarchism has been also called "The Night Watchman state."

Ironically, the term "night watchman" to describe this was originally used to mock the limited government stance. However, Ludwig von Mises decided that that was a great description because much like a night watchmen only concerns himself with protecting the store from intruders and thieves, the government should likewise only concern themselves with protecting the citizenry from those wishing to steal their freedoms. This is in contrast, as Mises suggested, from a government that "concerned itself with the preparation of sauerkraut, the manufacture of trouser buttons, and the publication of newspapers".

Minarchists justify government only for the purposes of military, the police, and courts. Often they will extend those purposes to civil defence and emergency services like firefighters, prisons, and even the three branches of government that we are currently familiar with today. The free market would remain in tact, but it would add the protection of the courts as well as fire and police and military.

The minarchist justifies the existence of the state as a logical consequence of adhering to the non-aggression principle. Because by following the non-aggression principle, it would only be natural that rules would need to be made in order to set boundaries. And who would set those boundaries? Surely we would want the wisest and smartest people to make those rules, we can't have everyone making their own rules and people are expected to know them and follow them. So, you see, some semblance of a government would naturally arise, over time and as more issues arise.

Classical Liberals

The Classical Liberal has the unique distinction of being considered small government by modern mainstream politics while being considered big government in the libertarian circles. From our point of view, there is absolutely no difference between the Republican and Democratic Parties. They both engage in wasteful spending and meaningless politicking that distracts the country from the important issues. The Classical Liberal considers most functions of modern government completely unnecessary. While most functions of government are unnecessary, the only two functions that are absolutely necessary are defense from outsiders and settling internal disputes. Some of these functions are intertwined, which means one function will require another function to be adopted. But other functions are completely separate functions and should only be adopted if the State can properly perform this function. This brief essay will use the political chart in the beginning of the book as an outline.

To start this conversation we must realize that the Classical Liberal is different than the Anarchist in the fact that we realize that there must be a nation state, or state of some sorts for the purpose of defense from outsiders. Sure, there could be a non-professional militia that gets called up when an invading army approaches. But military history and philosophy has shown that non-professional militias are not the most efficient option for defending an invading army. One reason for this is that professional armies receive their wages for being a solider. In other words, a professional army does not have to be worried with the soldiers needing to leave their post to seek wages or tend to his private employment. If this standing army is to exist, which it should, then there must be some way to properly fund it. This calls for a tax. Realizing that the income tax is theft and the property tax is extortion, there must be some other way to fund the standing army. The purpose of this section is not to discuss taxes, so we will leave that subject until a later time.

Once this first function of a state is developed, as Classical Liberals we see the justification for the second function of the State to be development. Once the State is secure from outside aggression, perhaps even before, there will be a need for a system of settling internal disputes. An arbitrator could fulfill this role. As arbitrators are swapped out, there is no form of common law developed. Having a judge fill this role, there would be a set of common decisions or outcomes made involving cases. A common law would be formed. There would be a need for someone to enforce the decisions of the judge. This brings us to the marshal or constable. Again, this would have to be funded by some sort of tax, fee, or combination of the two. We see here that the creation of one function of government calls for another necessary role to be created. The constable/marshal is needed to support the authority of the judge. This growth of government, or assumption of power that we witness in this explanation is one of the rare legitimate cases of growing the size of government.

If corruption becomes an issue, which is likely since people are corruptible then there should be a method to remedy the situation. This brings us to a council or legislative body. The legislative body would be there to set guidelines and methods of accountability for the judge and his enforcers to comply with. The creation of the legislative body for this purpose presents the question of whether or not the professional military should answer to it. If you would like an unstable system, then no, the military should not be accountable to anyone. But it you want a state, then you would like for it to be stable. The funding and operations of the professional military would need oversight from the legislative body. After developing the legislative body we automatically see the opportunity for its power to expand. Would there be any need to expand the power of the legislature? If the purpose of the legislative body is limited to develop laws to protect the state, then there is either no need or little need for more powers to be given to it. If foreign relations and internal improvements are proper roles for the State, then assuming power over the roles is proper.

Foreign affairs are not necessarily an assumption of power for the legislature. If the legislature provides oversight and guidance to the military, then the legislature is already involved in foreign affairs. Should the legislature only be concerned with foreign affairs when there is war, or a war is imminent? To say this is indeed the proper role of the legislature would be a foolish mistake to make. Engaging in foreign affairs by utilizing ambassadors builds friendly relations with other states. Friendly relations bring trade, which benefits both states. Trade among states prevents wars. Trade among states allows luxuries and resources to trade hands. Engaging in foreign affairs is a necessary role for the state.

Internal improvements were a controversial subject in the early days of the United States under the current constitution. For the purpose of this conversation, we are not referring to federalism or the constitution. Along with the rest of the topic, we are speaking of general theory of the state. Should the state build a system of roads for the purpose of allowing the military to easily move from one portion of the state to another while engaging in defense? Should the state build a system of roads that promotes commerce within the state? Yes, this is legitimate function of government as long as there is adequate funding for it. Does this mean that the state shuts down the market and assumes a monopoly on these services? No, the state should never hold a monopoly over any service.

As we have seen, many functions of the state calls for a new function to be developed. This happens in layers. When adding a new layer, we must ask if it is necessary, as well as, affordable. Public education is an issue that Classic Liberals do not agree on. If we are to have a public education system, then we need to determine what the role of the government is, as well as, the funding mechanism. Remembering that the income tax is theft and property tax is extortion, those two are not an option. As far as the role of government in education, it must be limited to funding as well as stating what level of education is the minimum expected to be acquired. Developing curriculum and administering proficiency tests are not the proper role of government. Somehow, people have been led to believe that just because the government funds something, the government is somehow suddenly an expert in this area.

Being involved in more than what is discussed in this essay as well as what is shown in the chart shown earlier in the book is generally a bad idea. The state has a limited supply of funds, especially if the state respects people's income and property rights. Even more so, those funds are limited if the state violates these rights. Even if the state grabs every source of revenue that it can get its hands on, which is the current situation in the United States, there is still a limited amount of revenue. Once the state grows beyond the spectrum discussed, corruption becomes rampant. The rights of the people become oppressed. This is not a price that the Classic Liberal is willing to pay for "free" stuff.

The only legitimate roles of the state are to provide defense, the protection of rights, and the survival of a state. The more the state grows the more difficult this becomes. This is why we must ask if every function of the state is necessary or unnecessary. And by necessary, this is not whether or not someone likes or benefits from the function. If the state cannot afford to perform one of its roles, then the state does not perform the role.

PART II
Economic Issues

Corporatism, Cronyism, and Lobbyists

Current politicians like to talk about the American "free market" and "capitalism" like they know what they are talking about. The truth of the matter is, outside of Ron and Rand Paul, no modern politician really understands what those terms ACTUALLY mean. Before we dive into what a "free market" really looks like and how it functions, let's take it a look at what Americans THINK is free market capitalism.

What is Corporatism?

First, let's start at the top: The Mega-Corporations. Think of the conglomerate banks that begged Congress for a bailout. Here's the real kicker: Shortly after the crash of the toxic asset program, Congress presented a bill called the TARP Bill. It was over 1,000 pages and was released within 7 - 10 days of the crash. TARP stood for Toxic Asset Relief Program. It was pitched to the electorate as being helpful to the people who were hurt. However, there are some things that were troubling in that bill.

How did they write 1,000 pages in less than 2 weeks?

Aside from that, there were protections for the banks deeply embedded within the bill that took all liability off of the banks and put it directly onto the taxpayers. This is not new, it was set in motion when the Federal Reserve was put into place in 1913. It was designed to protect the banks from insolvency if there was a market crash. The problem with this is that students of the free market understand that market fluctuations are natural because depressions and recessions are the market trying to correct itself to its natural cycle.

The point is, when large corporations use their money and influence to dictate legislation or even write legislation that gets passed by Congress it positively affects the corporation that is pushing it. Large corporations are usually engaged in an activity called "bundling". It's a process that enables campaign contributions that exceed the standard maximum allowable donations set forth by the Federal Election Commission. When that happens, MILLIONS get raised immediately for a candidate. Human nature shows that even genuine people will show their appreciation to people who have done grand or immeasurably nice things for them. So it only stands to reason that while in office, a candidate who received large sums of money from corporate interests would seek to ensure those interests are happy so that when they need to run for re-election or a higher office, that those big money donors are still there.

Republican Presidential Candidate and Celebrity Businessman Donald Trump was criticized for donating heavily to more Democrats than Republicans over the last several years, he basically said, "I like to win, I was backing winning horses in case I ever needed a favor." Even the Republican presumptive nominee knows that politicians are beholden to those who give them large sums of money. This is the practice of corporatism. Corporations donate heavily to political campaigns for the sole purpose of effecting legislative change to the environment of the industry in which those corporations operate, thereby inherently giving themselves a leg up over the competition, and in some cases, like Wal-mart, using it for the purpose of crushing the competition.

In the first term of President Obama, all political battles were being waged either to garner support for or against the American Accountability and Affordable Healthcare Act (better known by the media as "Obamacare"). Wal-Mart was one of the early corporate supporters of Obamacare, and they encouraged their employees to contact their Congressmen and tell them to support Obamacare. This encouraged the employees of Wal-mart. The employees felt that Wal-mart was wanting to help them get affordable health care and that they and their family would be covered by an affordable plan offered through their employer. Once

Obamacare passed, many employees lost their health insurance through Wal-mart. Many others lost their jobs or had their hours decreased to below 30 hours per week in order to comply with new definitions that state full-time employment is working more than 30 hours per week (overtime still starts after 40 hours).

In a letter from "Wal-mart Friends" to their shareholders they said that they are for "shared responsibility", but that has nothing to do with it. While Wal-mart cited that had they not dropped coverage eligibility by the end of Jan 2015, their health insurance program would increase to over $500 million. However, that's disingenuous of Wal-mart. What they aren't saying is that they can opt not to provide health insurance to their employees and just pay the fines. Wal-mart employs 1.4 million people, they are America's largest employer. If they shaved all but 10% of their employees down to below "full-time equivalent", then that leaves 140,000 employees that they would have to cover. If they simply paid the $2,000 fine per employee not offered insurance, the fine would be $280 million. So, by paying the fine and dropping all insurance for all employees, Wal-mart then stood to gain an extra $220 million from the anticipated health insurance premium increases that would have had to otherwise pay.

So, why then did Wal-mart support Obamacare if they had no intention of being a good employer and offering (what was expected) to be more affordable options? Strategically speaking, to crush the competition. As stated, Wal-mart is the single largest private employer in America. They didn't get that way by having a handful of stores. Wal-mart has regularly been criticized that when they enter a market, local chains and small "mom and pop" operations suffer and eventually close. So while Wal-mart has already taken down smaller operations, their support of Obamacare would help to hurt their larger competitors like Kroger. By being able to afford to pay the fines by not offering health insurance, Wal-mart execs knew that their competitors couldn't afford to do the same, therefore they would have to seek to cut their workforce down significantly, and one sure-fire way of doing that: layoffs and store closures. While Kroger was able to survive, many smaller chains were not, or they sold out to Kroger or Wal-mart (for use as their new "Neighborhood Market" concept).

All in all, this was an example that Wal-mart, who traditionally backs Republican candidates, supported the Democrat-heavy bill, for the purpose of benefiting their corporation. While they did nothing illegal or immoral, they did so with the purpose knowing it would harm their employees the most. This is Corporatism in a nutshell.

Crony Capitalism, or Cronyism

In order to fully understand what cronyism is, let's provide a hypothetical. The mayor of a city is best friends with a contractor in town. The city needs to build a new wing to the public library. Whereas typically the city officials get bids for any jobs that the city is going to pay; however, the mayor convinces the board of supervisors to hire his friend to do the work. No bidding process, no reference checking, just hired. The board is urged that all will be fine, he's a good contractor, he won't cost us too much. Then the project goes over time and over budget.

This happens at all levels of government from your local town all the way to the federal government. Think back to after the "surge" into Iraq. American forces toppled Saddam Hussein's regime and fought against the insurgents. After it was declared Iraq "safe" for the most part, then we practiced "Nation building". First we sent in contractors, but rather than go through the lengthy bidding practice, they just turned to then Vice President Dick Cheney and had him mobilize his Halliburton workforce. While Cheney was not President/CEO of Halliburton, he was on the board and had financial interest in the company.

This move benefitted the company to the tune of nearly $40 BILLION in government contracts. This is great if you are an employee, because going to work in another country means more pay, then couple that with it being still a war zone means hazard pay. The problem was that cries of cronyism and conflict of interest fell on deaf ears for a vast majority of people.

I live on the Mississippi Gulf Coast, and we see this type of cronyism all too often. I have often said that Mississippi politics is run by the F.B.I...Friends, Brothers, and In-Laws. Sadly, this joke is not funny because it's true. Take, for example, the Hilton Hotel in Pascagoula, Mississippi. Now, Pascagoula is not a tourist location. There are some things to find there, but for the most part, it's a middle-class, blue-collar city. Home to Ingalls Shipbuilding and the Chevron refinery, there's not much "industry" there. While the crime rate has gone down through the years, it's still not a relatively safe place, especially when the sun goes down. But owners of the old La Font Inn didn't seem to think this was important when they decided to tear it down and build a new, state-of-the-art Hilton hotel.

That was two years ago, and news recently shows that it has not made a profit yet and there's talks that the taxpayers of Pascagoula may be on the hook for a loan that was made. "Wait...what?" I know...let's go back.

In 2012, the owners of the La Font Inn realized that it

would probably cost more to revamp and retrofit the decaying hotel than it would to build a new one...and they found a way to make that happen. They, with help from the City of Pascagoula, applied for Federal Grant money from HUD (Housing and Urban Development) through the Mississippi Development Authority. They received $3.3 MILLION that was used by the city to clear the grounds for the new hotel, fix the roads and utilities around the new area and get it ready for construction. Then the developers secured $6.5 million from investors (13 of which were foreign investors utilizing a little known loophole that allows foreign investors to get a green card if they invest $500,000 or more in impoverished areas. [See EB-5 Immigrant Investor Program - est. 1990].) With all that free money, it still wasn't enough apparently, and the developers secured a $5.2 million loan that includes tax credits and doesn't have to be paid off until 2052. That's a 50 year term!

Well, now in 2016, it appears that there's still a debt. The owners have asked for a loan from the City of Pascagoula to the tune of $1.36 million. The owners claim it is to reimburse developers for the "infrastructure"...WAIT! Didn't they get a $3.3 Million grant for "infrastructure"? Yes, they did, but the owners apparently aren't able to cash flow that amount owed, and therefore are returning with their hand out. The developer has claimed this property is a $20

million property. Interestingly enough, the entire property
with the old La Font Inn didn't even appraise for $500,000
(according to property records in the Jackson County Land
Records).

It doesn't matter if it's a BILLION dollar Federal
Contract or the small town goes with the brother of the
mayor to cut the town's grass. When a process is put into
place and that process is completely undermined by the
leaders in power, what's the point of a system? Cronyism
goes much deeper than just no-bid contracts. How many
times have we seen legislators get voted out of office and as
soon as their belongings are packed up they move right down
the road to K Street into the offices of Gett, Munny, & Run
Lobbist firm? Which takes us to the next point…

**Lobbyist: Or how to go from elected parasite to
high-paid leach**

Lobbying is a time loathed profession. Yes, there are
some "good" lobbyists, but all lobbyists represent special
interest groups that seek to get the government to give them
money or pass laws that are favorable to their interest group.
When I say "good" lobbyists, I mean those that represent
very altruistic groups like Muscular Dystrophy Association or
Children's Cancer Research. No one will argue that these are
groups that should receive more money to help research

efforts to fight against these horrible medical conditions.

Lobbying started, and got it's name, from the era of Teddy Roosevelt. Paid representatives from special interest groups (worker's rights, women's rights, etc) would pull members of Congress aside in the lobby of restaurants to talk to them about helping their cause, either through direct money or policy/law changes. However, the question that Libertarians want to know is "are lobbyists necessary?" The answer is simply, NO! When one understands that Libertarians neither support government regulating and controlling the actions of others nor do they support the government using money for any purposes, altruistic or other.

There's a great story that has been shared from the Foundation for Economic Education about then Representative Davy Crockett. In a nutshell, Davy Crockett gave a speech regarding his opposition to a bill that would have given a gift of $50,000 to the widow of a Navy Admiral that died of natural causes years after his retirement. Crockett explained that he was educated by a farmer in his district to the radical notion that the government's money "is not yours to give." It shocked Crockett and he vowed to that farmer, along with all constituents in his district that he would seek to protect their money, no matter how much it was. At the end of his speech he pledged one week's salary to the donation to the Navy Admiral's widow and urged the others to do the same. The bill failed and all representatives donated one week's salary and it ended to be more than they were ready to give.

Let me provide another example from American history where an elected official protected the American taxpayers over the interest of the other elected officials. The year was 1887, and a devastating drought impacted the farmers in Texas to what would now probably be called "State of Emergency" levels. The problem was that they did not know if they would be able to produce enough crop for market AND for seed the following year. So Texas Congressmen drafted a bill that flew through both houses of the legislature and landed on the desk of President Grover Cleveland. The bill, by today's standards, asked for a mere $10,000 (even meager by today's dollars, less than $300,000 after adjusting for inflation.) Pres. Cleveland vetoed the bill, but gave a statement regarding why he vetoed. He said:

I can find no warrant for such an appropriation in the Constitution; and I do not believe that the power and duty of the General Government ought to be extended to the relief of individual suffering which is in no manner properly related to the public service or benefit. A prevalent tendency to disregard the limited mission of this power and duty should, I think, be steadily resisted, to the end that the lesson should be constantly enforced that, though the people support the Government, the Government should not support the people.

That's right, he put it on the PEOPLE of America to support the farmers. And do you know what...they DID! Donations from around the country started flowing in and when it was all said and done they received over 6x the amount that Congress laid out.

I know...I know, what does this have to do with lobbyists? Simply to explain to you that there was a period of time that our elected officials did not believe in spending taxpayer money on things that they did not deem as "constitutional duties" as Cleveland put it. "But don't lobbyists help a lot of people?" Sure, mainly themselves. If they have even a 5% fee on the money raised through Congress, then when Congress funds cancer research to the tune of $5 BILLION per year and much of that initiated by lobbyists, their firm might get up to $250 MILLION. Which if you believe in the cancer research, then the lobbyists just took $250 million from curing little kids.

We have to get to a point in American society that we begin to return to our original roots, caring about our fellow man. While many socialists will make the argument that the government has a bigger purse to play with than the common man...sure. And when I get my paycheck I don't see my share of that altruism, I just see FICA on my pay stub. However, it seems that number goes up and up every year.

True, the average American doesn't feel the direct impact of each of the programs of the government and we'll get to more about that in the "Taxation is Theft" chapter; right now we are merely focused on the masterminds of the thieves. Let's go back and look at the Toxic Asset Relief Program (or TARP) that followed the market crash of 2008. Within 2 weeks there was a bill presented before Congress that was over 1,000 pages. How? How was this even possible? OKAY TIN FOIL HAT WARNING! Because there were people who saw it coming!

Go ahead! I'll wait for your shock to wear off...

Okay, now that you're back. It's true. In fact, President Bush and several Congressmen, including Ron Paul, had been warning about the practice that started during the Clinton administration that Fannie Mae and Freddie Mac (largest grantors of home loans) was dangerously insolvent because of the number of bad loans they purchased. WHAT

HAPPENED EXACTLY?

Since the 1970's the government has increased both
funding and expansion of federal housing initiatives, designed
to create more homeowners. This caused an artificial bubble
in the housing market and a 40 year rise in home prices.
Couple that with subprime mortgages (created again by
government policy) and you have now encouraged banks to
make riskier loans more frequently. This built a house of
cards scenario for banks that crumbled under the weight of
bad loans predicated on bad government policies.

In a nutshell, lobbyists exist for one reason and one
reason only: to get as much taxpayer money for the cause or
industry they have been paid to support. They are literally the
parasites that feed off the lifeblood that is the taxpayers. A
lobbyist is only loyal to the cause because they are getting
paid. They are political mercenaries, who will work for the
highest bidder. And politicians are no different, since they
spend more of their time getting re-elected than actually
understanding the system upon which this great nation was
founded.

Free Trade and World Peace

Americans live under the delusion that we practice free trade, however, that is not the case. Free trade would indicate that we trade freely with all nations in the world; but however we have embargoes on other nations and tax penalties for businesses that operate from within those countries or does business through other countries that don't have embargoes with the "enemy" countries. So how would free trade bring world peace? Let's dive into how free trade would work.

To begin, this assumes that there are little barriers to entering the marketplace, which currently is not the case in America. What is Free Trade, exactly? Simply put, no tariffs or barriers to sell a product or service to anyone from America or in America. Take what's been going on with Cuba. President Obama has called for a softening of the travel and trade embargo with Cuba. This is a major step toward two things: American business growth and Cuban business growth.

The Cuban Market

With businesses being allowed into Cuba, the Cuban people will benefit by new products and services. And when you consider that Cubans drive 50's era cars because they have old car factories with the original dies and presses, the vintage car market in America will benefit by getting original body pieces rather than aftermarket parts. Opening trade benefits both countries, and for American entrepreneurs, the sky is virtually the limit because the embargo on Cuba has been in place for over 60 years.

Why this matters…

As the Castro regime begins to change hands from Fidel to his brother and sons, enabling the Cuban people to have more freedom to choose different products and services opens the world to them when they were once behind the times, technologically speaking. Much like what has been happening in China, with the rise of Capitalist practices, the Chinese people are beginning to see their world open up to them more. As they get more tastes of freedom, they will continue to seek more and more liberties until the Chinese people use their collective voices to seek new political powers. The same thing will happen with Cuba, but it might not take as long for the Cuban people since many of them clamor to get to America, even risking their lives.

How will this bring about world peace?

If other countries and their economies were

dependent upon American products and services then their governments would be less likely to rock the boat. As American companies grow, other countries will follow suit in doing business in these countries. Since the end of the cold war, we shifted the principle of Mutually Assured Destruction to Mutually Assured Economic Destruction. All our nations economies are tied together. We saw this play out a few years ago when Greece began to fall and the European Union was scrambling to stop the bleeding and prevent other countries from experiencing similar economic meltdowns.

No, I'm not saying that connecting our economies together is a good thing, but each country benefiting from free and open trade with the world will improve the economies around the world. The phrase from the era of Reaganomics (while flawed in many areas) does hold true, "the rising tide lifts all boats."

Minimum Wage is Racist

When the Minimum wage law was first enacted, it was pushed by the unions for the purpose of preventing many of the blacks from being able to offer their labor for a much lower wage. So the entire intent was racist, and it remains so to this day. While lawmakers try to explain that a higher minimum wage must be passed in order to help the minority community, the fact remains that black unemployment (in 2015) was 9.5% for those with only a High School diploma or GED. Compared to White unemployment in the same category, blacks are unemployed at more than twice the level of whites. Why is that, do you suppose? Are blacks lazy, as the racists would say. I have heard that they all just want to be basketball stars or rappers. While I know some that would fit that category, I know many more that do not. In fact, in my personal experience, I know more blacks that are harder workers than whites. But work ethic is not a race issue, it's personal.

But let's do an experiment, think of this as part of Economics 101. A job opens at a fast food restaurant and two people have applied. The first being Lester, a 30 year old black man and former drug addict who just been released from jail after stealing from his previous employer. He assures the manager that he has seen the error of his ways and wants to make a new start to life. Then the second is Chad Alexander Smith, a 20 year old white college student who pulled into the parking spot in a BMW and walked into the restaurant like he owned the place wearing a tailored suit. He's never had a job, and wanted to make some honest money.

While most people would be willing to take the risk on Lester, the truth is that because Lester cannot negotiate that he would be willing to work for less money or in a riskier position, he has nothing with which to bargain with in order to make him the favored applicant. Naturally, Chad gets the job. Even if this was based on race, the owner of the restaurant is shielded from any real scrutiny because of his bigotry by defending his choice by saying that Chad was the better applicant and would be easier to train.

Had Lester had the ability to negotiate by telling his potential employer that he would work for $5.00 per hour and would be willing to work 50 hours per week without overtime, then Lester might have gotten the job, and if he didn't because the owner was racist, then the owner's bias would be exposed and the business would most likely suffer significant damage to the bottom line. However, because there was no legal ramifications for Lester, the owner could essentially be as racist as he wanted in his hiring decision. Completely protected by the law, and pushing Lester back to the outer fringes of society.

I hear what you are saying, "But who would work for $5.00 per hour?" Not many, but there would be those that choose to, whether as part of negotiating because they know that their history might affect employment or because they don't need a lot of money, maybe a second job, or any number of reasons. This could be easily part of the negotiating process during hiring. With minimum wage being the expectation, the only way the EMPLOYERS can compete for better quality employees is by offering benefits; medical, 401k, etc. This is more important in today's world to a vast majority of workers than money. If someone knows that they have employer-paid health insurance (with Dental...BONUS), they might consider working for minimum wage in exchange for premium benefits and simply accept that they might need to get a second job in order to make more money, but they will keep and perform as best as possible just to keep the benefits.

Despite the inaccurate reporting of the unemployment number, Americans are not working as they used to. And when you have "Whopper floppers" lobbying for $15.00 per hour, it is clear that they do not understand economics or how they are perpetuating a cycle that will cause more and more minorities to become unemployed or unemployable.

Taxation is Theft

If I were to begin this section on Taxation, I could sum it up in three words: TAXATION IS THEFT. But I know many of you would like a deeper explanation (even for a "Nutshell" book). So let's consider for a moment that prior to 1913, Government still operated, we had a military, we had roads and schools...but the concept of a Federal Income Tax was considered "unconstitutional." Let's look at WHY a direct tax on the people was unconstitutional.

> Article I, Section 9
>
> *No capitation, or other direct, tax shall be laid, unless in proportion to the census or enumeration herein before directed to be taken.*

So, the Constitution expressly forbid Congress from direct taxation either by "capitation" (or Poll tax of non-property owning citizens) or upon their income UNLESS Congress takes IN EQUAL PROPORTION of the number of people in an area OR by giving a detailed accounting of who and how much will be taken.

A Quick Legal History of Taxation in America

This lasted for awhile, until the Revenue Act of 1861, which levied on the higher earning individuals: 3% on those earning above $600 but less than $10,000; 5% on those earning $10,000 or more. It was repealed and replaced with the Revenue Act of 1862, then later by the Revenue Act of 1870 (which Congress let the law expire in 1873). However, some provisions still remained until the law was challenged in 1880 by Mr. Williams Springer when he sued the US Government in Springer v. United States, where he asserted that a tax upon his business earnings and bond interest income violated the "direct tax" clause in Article I, Section 9.

Unfortunately for Mr. Springer, the Supreme Court ruled that the tax was neither a capitation (populate/poll tax) nor was it property tax, and therefore did not violate the Direct Taxation clause. This held until 1894, where Congress passed the Wilson-Gorman tariff. This levied the first peacetime income tax of 2% on all people earning more than $4,000 per year. It is interesting to note that Wilson-Gorman was passed without President Cleveland's signature (meaning he vetoed and Congress overruled the Veto.)

In 1895, along comes Mr. Pollock, who had some investments in land as well as was a farmer, sued the government saying that his investments on income from the production of his real estate was a direct tax and fails the Article I, Section 8 taxation clause that requires all "duties, impost and excise taxes to be apportioned among the several states." The court agreed with him and partially overturned Springer v US and ruled that a direct taxation on income and on real property was deemed unconstitutional...and it remained that way for about 15 more years.

By 1909, Congress passed the Sixteenth Amendment which states *"The Congress shall have power to lay and collect taxes on incomes, from whatever source derived, without apportionment among the several States, and without regard to any census or enumeration."* And by February of 1913, was ratified by enough states to officially become an Amendment to the Constitution. Congress reassured the public that this tax would be ONLY for the upper 1% of income earners. That lasted 8 years, then it was applied to everyone.

It's also important to note, that in 1913 something more sinister and devious was created, but not in Washington, DC, but rather Jekyll Island, Georgia. The same year that the Income Tax became part of the Supreme Law of the Land, the Federal Reserve Bank was created along with what would become the Federal Deposit Insurance Company (FDIC). In short, the largest banks at the time wanted protection against runs that would drain their deposits and cause the banks to fail. So, with the help of Congress, the Federal Reserve was created, along with a company that would insure banks deposits: should something befall the bank, with taxpayer money. Basically, the large banks at that time are still in existence because the Government PROTECTED the banks by promising to cover their losses due to theft or runs. This is what it means when your bank says they are "FDIC Insured."

So, now taxation is Constitutional, right?

Legally, yes. But Americans, especially in modern America, have a very short memory span, this is how Congress' approval rating is nearly in the single digit range while maintaining a 96% re-election percentage. Let's break it down. If I told you that you MUST work for me for 40+ hours per week, but I will give you a place to live, provide you with minimal sustenance, and give you clothes that no longer fit me, you would tell me to go screw myself. GOOD! You should, because that's how the slaves were treated. That is 100% of the theft of another man's labor. So this begs the question, what percentage of theft of another man's labor is not slavery? In 2016, April 24th marks "Tax Freedom Day". Tax Freedom Day is the day where the total incomes of American workers is equal to the total amount of Tax that will be taken by the Government for that year. In short, nearly 4 months of your life in 2016 is spent covering your portion of the American income tax.

Now, honestly, this number is (while calculated) merely arbitrary. Because the only way that this could TRULY be Tax Freedom Day is if the first 4 months of your income went to the government directly and then the remaining months you do not pay any more taxes. Of course, they would not do this because...well, the people would revolt. So they spread it out over the 12 months, and if you didn't pay enough, you have to write them a check. If you paid too much, then they give you a refund...or more accurately, your change.

While most Classical Liberals do not mind taxation for "necessary" items, they do care about their money going to entitlement and other failed government programs. And when you include corporate welfare into the mix, we really don't like that. It's one thing to allow a business to do business with the government, it's a totally different thing to prop the business up because you find them "too big to fail." Big government supporters love to point out that the income tax is voluntary. However, it is not. I cannot get a job without paying taxes...well, okay, I can, but if the government ever found out that I was earning money without reporting it, they would arrest me for tax evasion. But when you consider that there are over 11,000 pages in the tax code (in six volumes of books) devoted SOLELY to Income Tax Regulations, tell me that you haven't accidentally evaded taxes.

It is interesting to note that at the fall of the Soviet Union, when the Russians were trying to figure out the best system of governance for themselves, they implemented American-style progressive income taxes. Within 2 years they changed to a flat tax because they said that a tax structure like America would lead to corruption. Can we all just pause for a moment while we facepalm ourselves?

As our government increases its size and scope in order to "protect the children/American people/etc.," the truth is, the American people do not need to be protected from anything that doesn't physically harm us or takes our property. But what happens when the government is the biggest perpetrator of taking our property in the form of taxation. The problem with taxation (aside from everything) is that those that support things like universal healthcare, a "living wage", and even guaranteed income, are opposed to things like defense funding. And those that support defense funding and corporate tax credits are opposed the universal healthcare and a "living wage." So, when our government tries to balance these interests it always seems to increase expenses, which in turn will increase taxes that are needed for those expenses.

Remember: before the government can give $1 to someone, they must take $1 from someone else. The basic functions of government, as stated by the Constitution are: to protect the country; quell rebellions; foreign relations; and settle disputes between the states. The question is, how to pay for it? So, what would a libertarian taxation plan look like? The limitations are simple, no direct taxation on personal income.

Ideally, a Libertarian would want no taxation on a person's income or property. However, a Classical Liberal recognizes that there needs to be some semblance of government, if for nothing else than for the military. In fact, the often cited Article I, Section 8 of the Constitution of the United States clearly states what authority Congress has with regards to laying and collecting taxes: *"The Congress shall have Power To lay and collect Taxes, Duties, Imposts and Excises, to pay the Debts and provide for the common Defence and general Welfare of the United States; but all Duties, Imposts and Excises shall be uniform throughout the United States"* however, as mentioned earlier, Article I, Section 9 limits the Constitutional powers of Congress, but then again the 16th Amendment DID render Section 9's limit moot.

A Libertarian tax would be a tax that would return the power of the Federal budget back to the states. While this is "in a nutshell", this particular topic is too detailed to get into all the nuances of a real Libertarian Plan, but it MUST include the repeal of the 16th AND 17th Amendments. The 16th Amendment created the Income Tax, whereas the 17th

Amendment allowed for a popular vote of Senators. Prior to the 17th Amendment, the State Legislature was responsible for appointing Senators.

Why is the State appointing Senators important? Do they do their job differently?

Actually...yes! By being appointed by the State Legislature, they are the STATE's voice in the Federal Government. (Side note: The term "national" applies to the nation, as a whole; the term "federal" indicates a gathering of independent states for the purpose of governing.) The Federal government operated completely different before then. Oddly enough, the ratification of the 17th Amendment also followed the ratification of the 16th Amendment...hmm. That should make people wonder why???

So...why?

Prior to the ratification of the 16th and 17th Amendment, taxation was limited and so was the Federal Government. The Federal government would offer up a Budget, then once the Budget made its way to the Senate, the Senators would find out what the apportioned amount was for their state and report back to the State legislature. If the state could afford the apportioned taxation, then the legislature would instruct the Senators to return to DC with a

"Yes" vote on the Budget. IF the state could not afford, or just didn't like items within the budget, they instructed the Senators to vote "No" on the budget, thereby giving the State the ability to control the taxation that was received by the people of the state TO the Federal government. This was the way that it had been since the ratification of the Constitution in 1788. And it worked fairly well, until the early part of the 1900's. By that time, America was considered a Superpower and our influence among the nations of the world was beginning to be wielded by politicians. More power requires more money.

So...what tax would a libertarian support?

A Libertarian would, and should, support any tax plan that intends to take as little money from the people and as much power from the Federal government. We can discuss the details later, but for right now, the Progressive income tax that we have is no longer working properly. It is used as a weapon against political opponents and as a favor machine for political allies. If the IRS wants to increase its revenue collection, before it turns its sights on the people, it should first look into the men and women who "run" this country. I will close this section with a quote. Charlie Rangle, former Chairman of the Ways and Means Committee (the people that write the tax code) remarked on his publicly exposed tax issues saying, "[the] tax code is too damn complicated." The man in charge of writing the tax laws said he failed to report rental revenue from an offshore real estate holding to the tune of $75,000 in taxes owed because the "tax code is too damn complicated." I think that says everything we need to know.

More Legalized Theft

Eminent Domain

The dictionary defines *eminent domain* as "the right of a government or its agent to expropriate private property for public use, with payment of compensation." Before we dive into the fact that a government only has allowances, not rights, let's take a brief tour of how eminent domain came about. The practice of eminent domain was included in early colonial Common Law, however, when it came time to address it in the Constitution, feelings had changed.

While most people understand that the fifth amendment protects against self incrimination and double jeopardy, the closing of the amendment states "...nor shall private property be taken for public use, without just compensation." In the early days of the United States, the only time that eminent domain was used was for the purpose of condemning property unsuitable for habitation. However, over the years, governments have found that they are able to take property that is necessary for "public" use and demolish a building to build a park or a road.

However things changed in 2005 with the court case of *Kelo vs New London*. In *Kelo*, the Supreme Court upheld that the town of New London, Connecticut, could use eminent domain for economic development purposes. What this means is that the state can take private property from one party and sell it to another party, presumably for the purpose of improving the overall quality of the state.

Before you start to defend Eminent Domain, think about how you would feel if it were your property. What eminent domain will do is use the force of the courts to rip the deed from your possession, force a check that the State deems to be "fair", and then sells the property to a private developer. Imagine that you are living on the land that your great grandfather passed down the line to you. Then a oil company wants to build a pipeline that will run right through your property. You offer to lease the land for a 50 year lease at a discount, they say "No." Is it right for them to be able to go to the County or State and ask them to take your property and sell it to them?

Civil Asset Forfeiture

Civil Asset Forfeiture has become something that is being exposed more and more often for its corruption in the program. It is a process by which a law enforcement agency (from city police to Federal agents) can legally take your property that MIGHT have been purchased with funds from illegal activities (i.e. selling drugs, prostitution, insider trading, etc). The insidious part of Civil Asset Forfeiture laws is that a conviction is not necessary for the State to profit from the sale of these seized assets. Assets can range from bank accounts, cars, boats, houses, electronics, etc., really nothing is off limits. And it can all be taken WITHOUT A CONVICTION.

State and local authorities have been using this as a secondary source of revenue for years. Then the federal government decided they wanted a piece of the action. Now, to limit the negative attention that local authorities receive for their participation in theft, the Justice Department set up a program that they will take a portion of the assets, sell them for the local authorities, then return a portion of the money.

Put this into another context: revenue from illegal activities is spread across legitimate businesses, and returns the bulk of the money to the principle. The government would call this type of activity "laundering". This is illegal if it is performed by you or me, but when the government does this it's called "fighting the war on drugs". Just because we are "at war" with something doesn't mean that you get to break the laws; I'm pretty sure that on a REAL battlefield, there are things called "rules of engagement" and if you break them, you are opening yourself up for criminal charges, court martial, or even death sentence.

In all cases, before you go off defending this practice of "lawful theft", ask yourself the following questions:

- Would I steal from this person for my benefit?
- Would I hire someone to steal from this person for my benefit?
- Would I advocate that others hire someone to steal from this person for my benefit or the "Greater Good"?

If you can answer "No!" to all of these questions, then you cannot support eminent domain or civil asset forfeiture, no matter how laudable they say it is. Remember, theft is theft no matter WHO does the stealing or by what methods.

PART III
Social Issues

"There Ought to Be A Law"

As a libertarian, one of the most frightening or worrisome things to hear is "there ought to be a law." When someone says that there ought to be a law against something, they usually do not put much thought into it. What if we took a moment to think about what it meant? We want a particular activity (collecting rainwater on private property, drinking raw milk, wearing sagging pants, insert an activity that you do not like here, etc) to be outlawed. If someone engages in this activity, then we have him or her fined for doing so. What happens if the person decides not to pay a fine over something that should not be illegal? An arrest warrant is issued. The police then search for the person to put them in jail. When the police find the person, the arrest begins to happen. And if the person decides that this entire thing is foolishness and will not be imprisoned for engaging in this activity that someone thought should be outlawed, the police escalate force. As a policeman escalates force for the purpose of enforcing an unjust law, the person has the right to defend himself. As the person defends himself, the policeman may feel that he is now being threatened, which will cause him to escalate force. This can get out of hand very quickly. The end result being that someone can be killed. Often times it is the one that is accused of a crime.

This is not said to motivate the anti-cop movement. This is to point out a flaw in the system. If something is not worth going through this scenario, then there probably should not be a law against it. Whatever the issue is that you think should be illegal, run it through this scenario. If you don't think it is right for something like this to happen over a certain issue (not paying library fines, using medical marijuana, drinking a 32oz soda, etc.) then you should not support a law making it illegal to engage in the activity. If the crime (crime meaning there is an actual victim) is serious enough to warrant this possible scenario then proceed with supporting the law.

The Right to Bear Arms

The *right to bear arms* is a controversial subject. Those on the Left think that they can infringe on this *right* while denying that their actions are indeed an infringement. Those on the Right think that they are supporting the *right to bear arms* by maintaining the progress of the Left instead of overturning it. Both groups are wrong. Some people will also say that the *right to bear arms* is about personal defense. They too are wrong. Not only is the *right to bear arms* a controversial subject, when understood by the original meaning, most people would be uncomfortable with it. It is time to have that conversation.

The *right to bear arms* as defined by the 2nd Amendment is to recognize that the citizens (the People) have the right to overthrow the government if the government becomes corrupt. When a politician states that he supports the 2nd Amendment, he is stating that he believes that you have the right to ensure that your rights are not violated by the government. When a politician states that he does not support the 2nd Amendment, he is stating that you do not have the right to ensure that your rights are not violated by a corrupt government. At what level of corruption the government must be at before this right is exercised has never been discussed. Whether or not it is appropriate to take up arms against the government if they take out a loan in your name and give the money to someone else, imprison a person that committed no crime, or some other offense is not the purpose of this conversation. We will simply skip over the "when is it appropriate" portion of the conversation and go to the portion of "it's time".

Western society was founded on the principle of overthrowing oppressive regimes. From the Magna Carta to the Declaration of Independence we see people throwing off the shackles of oppressive regimes. The only way that this can be done is if the People have access to the same type of weapons that the military has access to. By same kind of weapons, I mean conventional weapons. The discussion of whether or not civilians should have access to weapons of mass destruction is just complete nonsense. The improper storage of biological, chemical, or nuclear weapons can pose a serious threat to the health of the surrounding area. Besides, the likelihood of the United States government using any of these against the populace is between slim and none. There is no intellectual justification to further this portion of the conversation, so we will move on.

If the purpose in preserving the *right to bear arms* in the sense of the 2nd Amendment is to overthrow an oppressive regime, would it be appropriate for the oppressive regime to regulate this *right*? Would it be appropriate for the oppressive regime to determine who may have the ability to exercise this *right*? Would it be appropriate for this oppressive regime to limit one's ability to exercise this *right*? If it would not be appropriate for an oppressive regime to do this, would it be appropriate for a friendly regime to engage in these activities? If so, at what point would it be best to recognize that the friendly regime is not leaning toward the friendly side anymore? If the friendly regime is indeed leaning toward unfriendly, at what point would it be best to remove this power from the regime due to fear of the regime becoming unfriendly, or even oppressive? Allowing a regime to become corrupt or oppressive is too late to take away the power to regulate the *right to bear arms*, so the power should be removed before this transition happens. If an oppressive, corrupt, or unfriendly regime cannot be trusted, then it would be best to not let them have this power to begin with. It would be best to not allow any regime to regulate this *right*.

Some would argue that an unregulated *right to bear arms* could be dangerous. This is why we need the government to regulate and infringe on this right. We have already concluded that it is a conflict of interest for the government to regulate the *right to bear arms*. With that being said, we have to discuss how to keep guns out of the hands of those that are too dangerous to have them. Simple. If someone is so dangerous to society that they cannot be trusted with a firearm, then the person should not be walking around freely in society. In other words, the person should be locked up. Obviously this means that the person would have to be convicted of a crime. But that is the way this system is supposed to work. This would be a good time to make it clear that exercising the *right to bear arms* is not a crime.

As was stated earlier, the Left thinks that they are permitted to infringe on this *right* by denying the ability to practice said right and/or by placing obstacles in front of citizens that choose to exercise this right. We have seen the Left ban "assault" weapons, handguns, make the process to purchase a gun stringent, and now they want to place new restrictions on the firearm industry. This war that the Left wages on the *right to bear arms* is something that is done in increments. Their ultimate goal is to disarm the People. If you would like to give them the benefit of the doubt, tell me why they have passed laws in the past that did outlaw gun ownership? Once you realize that their goal is to disarm the People, can you tell me why they would like to do this? Please do not tell me it is to make society safer. We see the most horrific acts of violence happen in gun free zones. Let's not insult anyone's intelligence by acting like the gun bans are to make unarmed people safer from an armed attacker.

The Right claims to be pro gun, whatever that is supposed to mean. They used the Left's anti gun stance as a rallying cry to get people to send them donations to their campaigns. This allows them to get reelected. As I mentioned earlier the Right only maintains the progress that the Left has accomplished. At the federal level this is true. At the state level things are changing. Some states are becoming more gun friendly as others are trying to be as anti-gun as possible. Why is it that some states can get away with infringing on the *right to bear arms*? If this were a state issue, then there would be some room for discussion on the matter. But the federal government guaranteed the *right to bear arms* in the 2nd Amendment. The federal government also guaranteed in the 14th Amendment that the States would not infringe upon any right guaranteed by the federal government.

With that being said, I have to ask…why has there not been one member of the House of Representatives to introduce articles of impeachment in support of the *right to bear arms*? If a federal judge has upheld a law that infringes on the *right to bear arms*, then the judge has committed an impeachable offense. The judge is supposed to uphold the Constitution, not mold it to fit his political beliefs. If a judge makes a change to the Constitution through a decision, then the judge has taken the role of the legislature. This amending of the Constitution through a Court's opinion also violates the separation of powers clause. In a scenario such as this, the Representative would have to defend the 2nd & 14th Amendments while defending the concept of separation of powers. When it comes to state and local laws, the 2nd & 14th Amendments also have to be defended. The guilty party in this scenario would be the governor who signed the bill into law, and anyone else that had a hand in violating the rights guaranteed by the Constitution, including the legislators that approved the bill.

The *right to bear arms* as it pertains to the 2nd Amendment is not about personal defense. The right to bear arms for personal defense is a 9th Amendment issues. These are two similar but distinct rights. It is easy to confuse the two, and there does seem to be some confusion over this matter amongst the populace and the state. The 9th Amendment states, "The enumeration in the Constitution, of certain rights, shall not be construed to deny or disparage others retained by the people." This means that just because a right is not listed, does not mean that the People do not have that particular right. Nowhere in the Constitution is the right to personal defense listed. Personal defense is not listed in the 2nd Amendment. The 2nd Amendment discusses the security of a free State, which means that the People may keep firearms for the purpose ensuring that their rights are secure against any unwanted oppression from government forces. Since the right to self-defense is not mentioned in the Constitution, it is a right guaranteed by the 9th Amendment. This stance is at odds with the conventional thinking of what the 2nd Amendment means.

The conventional philosophy for the *right to bear arms* is about self-defense. As we have discussed, this is correct if we are keeping the conversation within the boundaries of the 9th Amendment. As we shift the conversation to its proper context, we can now begin the discussion of the proper methods of regulating one's right to self-defense. Before we begin discussing in which ways it may be proper or improper for one to defend himself, we must ask by what moral authority we can assume this role. In other words, how can we justify infringing on one's natural law rights to self-defense? If your answer is that we took a vote and had more numbers for one position than the other, then you do not understand how rights work. Mere numbers are not justification for assuming authority of another person. In other words, there is no moral justification for regulating another person's right to self-defense.

Since the 2nd Amendment is about overthrowing an oppressive regime, a process should be put in place to address grievances by the regime. The Courts are the first thing that comes to mind. The Courts exist to address grievances by the government. If this were the purpose of the 2nd Amendment, then the Amendment would say, "in order to preserve the securities a system of courts will be established." But it does not say that. It speaks to a well-regulated militia being necessary. The 2nd Amendment was written with the assumption that the Courts were just as corrupt as the legislative and executive branches. With that being said, what is the ideal way to exercise 2nd Amendment rights? That depends on exactly what the grievance is.

If the grievance were one that does not include the immediate potential loss of life, then it would be appropriate to open up a form of dialogue before any action is taken. If the assembled militia addressed the responsible government entity that their actions are oppressive and that the continuation of said actions would result in the taking up of arms, then the government entity would have to make a decision. At this point there are only two options: the first being to meet the militia with force and the second would be to engage in dialogue. And by engaging in dialogue I do not mean shooting an unarmed person or burning a building full of men, women, and children. The purpose of the dialogue should be to determine if this situation warrants the taking of a life. Does the government entity believe that this action or policy is so detrimental to the safety of the community that they must take the life of the members of this militia? Or does the militia make a valid point? The idea that the militia should be arrested for assembling together and voicing their concerns is complete nonsense. Assembling a militia together is not illegal. It is a natural law right protected by the 2nd Amendment. When this right is exercised, it is the responsibility of the state to examine its own actions and policies to see if they are at fault. If they are at fault, then they should make the appropriate corrections.

If the state did take up a meaningful dialogue with an armed militia, some would be concerned that this could open up a can of worms. Some would say that this would infringe on the sovereignty of the state. This is not the case. The state is not all sovereign. The state gets its authority to govern from the governed. If the state becomes corrupt and infringes on rights, then it is the obligation of the People to exercise their 2nd Amendment rights. And if the 2nd Amendment is exercised, it is the obligation of the State to correct its own actions. But what if the militia is wrong? Well, democracy is a double-edged sword. It swings both ways.

The right to take up arms against a corrupt government is not some Revolutionary War mentality, because we had this very thing happen in modern America. Soldiers returning from World War II found that the city governments in Athens and Etowah, Tennessee, had become corrupt. The politicians had rules set for themselves and the Sheriff was in collusion with the corruption. The people encouraged the soldiers to run for office, which they did. On election day, before the ballots could be counted, Sheriff deputies stormed the voting precincts and took the locked ballot boxes and holed themselves up in the jail. The soldiers went to the local National Guard armory and were permitted to take weapons. They surrounded the jail, and exchanged fire with the Sheriff deputies. Only after explosives were used to blow open the door to the jail did any of the deputies surrender. The ballot boxes were retrieved, still locked, and then officially counted. All of the corrupt politicians and even the Sheriff were voted out of office overwhelmingly (to no one's surprise.)

The Right to Refuse Service

There has been some controversy as of late in regards to people being denied service due to the provider's religious beliefs. There are some that refuse to partake in certain activities because engaging in said activity would be a violation of the person's religious beliefs. Those on the opposing side are offended over the idea that a person could have not only have an opposing belief, but act on it. This discussion currently focuses on the religious aspect of the subject, but there is more to this topic. The subject of involuntary servitude has been overlooked in this discussion.

Regardless of one's view on gay marriage, or one's view on the Supreme Court assuming the role of the Congress by legislating, the Supreme Court has made a ruling that despite the bickering of the several of the States, the States will abide by the ruling and recognize gay marriage. The fact that the States are conforming to the wishes of an out-of-control federal government can only happen because the States look to Washington for funding. That subject can be discussed elsewhere. The point that we have to focus on for this current conversation is that the States are recognizing gay marriage as a legal entity. This change in policy has led to gay couples wanting to have ceremonies to celebrate their special moment of forming a union.

Just like with any other ceremony, there are special clothing purchases and event planning. This is a good economic opportunity for those who are willing to take it. But not all want to take advantage of this new economic opportunity. There are people that think that gay marriage is a violation of natural law. And natural law is not something that they would like to be in violation of. The phrase that is commonly used is, "against religious beliefs." For some this is an acceptable excuse. For others, it is an offensive excuse. To the libertarian it is an excuse that is not needed.

That is right, an excuse for refusing service is not required. Giving an excuse is a courteous act, but the excuse for refusal of service does not need approval from society or the government, especially the government. The reason for this is that each person is a sovereign entity. A sovereign entity, a sovereign person is not obligated to perform any duty or service for another person. In other words, a sovereign person is not bound to any form of involuntary servitude. At one time the federal government respected this idea by passing the 13th Amendment, which abolished involuntary servitude.

By invoking the 13th Amendment in this discussion, we have completely taken the need for the 1st Amendment out of the conversation, as well as, the 9th Amendment. We can discuss how those amendments would factor into the conversation should the Constitution be formally amended to change or abolish the involuntary servitude clause of the 13th Amendment. But for the time being, we will simply focus on the involuntary servitude portion of the 13th Amendment.

When the 13th Amendment was ratified, there was fear that the "freedmen" would be forced to stay on plantations and work for their former owners. This plight, if not prevented, would have done little to improve the situation of the "freedmen." If the freedmen were bound to one employer with no freedom to pursue their happiness, would they really be free? If the freedmen were bound to a group of employers, or could only choose employment from a limited group of potential employers, would they really be free? If the freedmen were able to pursue employment from any potential employer, but were obligated to perform acts of employment for anyone that demanded the freedmen to be an employee, would they really be free? Of course not. In order for a person to be free, the person must be able to turn down any employment that is not wanted. In order for a person to be free, the person must be able to pursue employment without being coerced into an organization, club, union or approval of another person. Abolishing involuntary servitude means that the individual is free to seek employment as well as turn down the opportunity for employment based on his own free will, not another's.

There is a growing hostility in this country toward religion, particularly one religion. Whether or not this is due to the culture wars is not the point of this conversation. The point is that regardless of how much the Left wants to hate this particular religion, the Left cannot make followers of this religion or any other religion engage in activities that the followers believe would be in violation of said religion. If involuntary servitude was once again allowed in this country, people could still deny service based on religious objections. The wall that was erected between church and state works both ways. The church cannot reach over and dictate what the state will do. And the state cannot reach over and dictate what the church will do. And by church this also applies to the followers of the religion, not just the institution itself (church meaning any religious institution).

Again for the sake of conversation we assume that involuntary servitude is once again allowed in this country. If this were the case, the People would still have their 9th Amendment right to conduct their business affairs in the manner that is in their best interest. The People would still have their 9th Amendment right to conduct their business in the manner that helps them pursue their happiness. Ninth

Amendment rights are rights that the People did not give up to the government. This is possible because our system is governed by consent. If someone did not consent to the government having power over this area, then it is still with the Person.

It is quite clear that a person has the right to deny service. When denying service, there is more than one right that the person may choose to exercise to justify this refusal. While denying service may cause an inconvenience for the customer, this is an inconvenience that must be dealt with if we are to be a free people.

The Drug War

The drug war is a noble program that is in place for the betterment of society. Well, that is what we have been told. The criminalization of drugs has enabled the cartels to make billions, made neighborhoods dangerous, and made a mockery of our criminal justice system. The way that the drug war has been fought has done more harm than good. It is time to reevaluate our approach to the epidemic use of drugs.

The beginning of this conversation is the appropriate time to divide drugs into two categories. In one category you have marijuana and in the other category you have the hard drugs. It's important to divide the two because they are two different subjects. The most dangerous thing about marijuana is getting caught with it while the most dangerous thing about the other drugs is using them. This is not to say that marijuana cannot cause harm in certain situations. But the mere causing of harm in certain situations is not justification for the criminalization of something that is far less dangerous than many of the prescription drugs and alcohol, which are legal.

The question must be asked, "Is the usage of marijuana or the hard drugs a crime?" By crime I mean, did someone's rights get violated? If someone lit up a joint or smoked some crack, did they violate someone else's rights? Did this action cause harm to someone else's body or property? If the answer is no, then there was no crime. A crime is only committed when someone's rights are violated or harm is done to them. Causing harm to yourself is not a crime. It may be stupid, but it is not a crime. In order for there to be a crime, there has to be a victim. This being the case, the drug laws should be overturned, or at the least amended.

Would it be appropriate to regulate the drug market? Sure, that is reasonable. This would fall under commerce, which the State does regulate. Would it be reasonable to have laws against manufacturing and distributing drugs? Absolutely. The State already takes measures to prevent harmful products to get to the market place. The difference here is that we are at a point where we have to decide what is more important; enforcing laws or dealing with health issues. Drug addiction is a health issue, not a crime. And it should be treated as a health issue, not a crime. That means that the focus should be on treatment, not arresting users.

Marijuana being a different issue, let us discuss it. If your teenage child gets arrested for having it, how many years would you like to see your child locked up? Probably none, especially since nothing wrong really happened. Maybe not an ideal situation, but definitely nothing worthy of prison. Is this an issue that you would prefer to deal with in a courtroom? Would you like to be at the mercy of a judge? Or would you prefer to take care of this issue at home?

Then there's the radical approach. Over a decade ago, Portugal legalized ALL drugs. Yes, you read that correct, ALL DRUGS...not just weed. Their approach was to address the real problem. Drugs are merely a symptom of the problem, but they recognized that ADDICTION is the real problem. So, they legalized everything and then used the money they were fighting the drug war with and funded addiction programs. While you won't catch a purist libertarian cheering on a government-funded program, at least this one actually sought to address the actual problem of addiction.

"I'm sure violence and addiction went through the roof, what with people no longer having to hide their usage and sneak around to get their drugs."

You would think that, at least that is what the Prohibitionists would have you believe: greater access to the drugs will increase the usage of those drugs. What Portugal saw was not the case. Addiction rates dropped by 50%. But the real interesting statistic comes from the 80% decrease in their crime rate.

"But...but most of the crimes that decreased were drug crimes."

Sure! But now police aren't chasing down teens with dime bags and instead are actually policing and solving IMPORTANT crimes, like burglary, homicide, and rape. So, there's another benefit to ending the drug war. Police will actually become more effective because they aren't chasing down the petty drug offenses and actually focusing on crimes where there is a real victim that has been physically harmed or had their property taken.

The height of irony, from the Federal Government, can be shown by pointing to US Patent No. 6630507 B1 (look it up.) Assigned to the United States of America "as Represented by the Department of Health and Human Services", the Patent Abstract reads:

> *Cannabinoids have been found to have antioxidant properties, unrelated to NMDA receptor antagonism. This new found property makes cannabinoids useful in the treatment and prophylaxis of wide variety of oxidation associated diseases, such as ischemic, age-related, inflammatory and autoimmune diseases. The cannabinoids are found to have particular application as neuroprotectants, for example in limiting neurological damage following ischemic insults, such as stroke and trauma, or in the treatment of neurodegenerative diseases, such as Alzheimer's disease, Parkinson's disease and HIV*

dementia.

Yes, you are reading that correctly, the Federal Government recognizes the medicinal benefits of marijuana by holding a patent on a compounded chemical while at the same time fighting against legalization of the same drug. This patent is not new, either, it was filed in 1998 and granted in 1999. So the federal government has literally held a patent PROVING that marijuana with high concentrations of cannabinoids have SIGNIFICANT medical benefits.

Restoring the Sanctity of Marriage

Marriage has a dual role in our society, society being modern day America. On one hand marriage is a covenant between two people (keeping it basic for now) and on the other hand marriage is a legal entity that is formed and regulated by the government. The covenant between two people is influenced by religions and philosophical beliefs. The legal entity that the state has formed was for the purpose of preventing some covenants from happening. Eventually the legal entity came with certain legal benefits. This dual role that marriage has become needs to be evaluated and the proper changes made to restore the sanctity of marriage.

Marriage has always been a relationship between two people. They start a family. The family gathers with other families and forms a township, tribe, or clan. A society is built from this. The family is the basic building block of society. From the family a set of beliefs is adopted and this develops a culture, a way of life for a people. Without a family, without this organic system a people cannot stand strong. Karl Marx realized this. He stated that after instituting the ten planks of the communist platform, the next step to establish a communist system is to destroy the traditional family and religion of a people. The reason that this is done is because family and religion are the ultimate forms of authority in a person's life. The goal of a communist state is to be that ultimate authority in a person's life.

There has been an effort as of late to have the government redefine what marriage is. So far this has been happening. There has also been an effort by those on the Left to redefine what a family is. We have government officials and politicians redefining the meaning of marriage and a family. This is dangerous ground that we are treading here. Do not be confused. I am not saying that the meaning of marriage cannot change. I am not saying that the makeup of a family can change. This can happen and has happened before. What I am saying is that when these changes do come, then the changes should be an organic change due to the behavior of people and society, not the government.

When the government, at the barrel of a gun, states what a marriage is then government assumes the role of a religious entity and/or a philosophical entity. This is not an appropriate role for government. For most people, marriage is a religious institution. The makeup of marriage as well as the purpose of marriage is determined by the religious beliefs.

Does government have the authority to cross over the wall of separation and mingle in the affairs of religion? For those that are not religious, they have philosophical beliefs concerning marriage. Even though philosophy is not held in as high esteem as religion is, philosophy is still important. If not given the same respect as religion, it should be held as somewhat sacred. A wall should also be built between the State and philosophy. The State should not cross over the wall and mingle in the affairs of philosophy. It is important to include philosophy in this conversation because of our atheist friends. Even though they are not religious, they do have deep moral convictions. Should their beliefs be disregarded because they are not religious? Not at all. We give their philosophy the same respect that we would like for them to give our religious beliefs.

If we recognize that there is a wall of separation between the state and religion/philosophy, the question must be asked, "Why do we allow the State to cross over the wall and regulate marriage?" Do we think that the state has authority over this issue? If so, then consider this. If the state completely banned marriage altogether, would you recognize the state's authority to do this? If not, on what grounds would your justification be? If you were fine with the state occupying the religious and philosophical sides of the wall, how can you object to the state exercising authority that you granted it? If you realize that you have made a mistake by inviting the state to come over the wall, then perhaps you should inform the state that it is no longer welcome to occupy this side of the wall.

Why is this being discussed now instead of at an earlier time? Is this because of gay marriage? Yes, and no. The LGBT community has demonstrated that we are not free in this area of our lives. This is not to say that they are right or wrong with their choices. This is to say that we have realized that there is a flaw in the relationship between the state and religion/philosophy. This flaw must be corrected. As Frederic Bastiat pointed out in The Law, when government abuses a power the only remedy is to remove the power from the government. In this case it means completely separating the state from marriage. If one objects to this because the government is already too involved in marriage, then it cannot be more clear that the government should move itself to the proper side of the wall. The only issues that should be remedied so that the State does not have any strings on this side of the wall are taxes, social security, and property issues. Concerning taxes, the income tax is still theft. It should be done away with. Concerning social security, if it was private property then people would be free to do with it what they will. Concerning property issues, a will, contract, or affidavit could be in place in case a dispute arose. There is clearly no need for the government to be involved in marriage. With there being no need, there is no reason for the government to stay on this side of the wall.

This is not an attempt to prevent the LGBT community from living their lives as they see fit. This is an attempt to allow people to rightfully follow their religious ideals as they see fit without any undue burden from other people. When someone from outside of your religious system steps in to dictate how your marriage is to operate and on what terms it can end, then your rights have been violated. Even if the person does have similar or the same religious beliefs, it is still not that person's place to assume this role. This role of forming the union and the one of being the one who dissolves the union can only be picked by those that are involved in the union. For the State to be involved in this process at all is an abuse of power.

Non-Intervention Foreign Policy

Libertarians prefer a non-interventionist foreign policy. Even though we do not call for isolating the country from others, we are accused of being isolationist for not wanting to use military force in place of diplomacy. I am not sure why they call us isolationists. I do not think that the Left or Right knows why they call us this. Since the Spanish American War the United States has become imperialistic. Since World War II the United States has become the policeman of the world. There is hardly a war that is not worth fighting. This costs money that could be better spent elsewhere as well as lives that are needlessly lost.

In the early days of the United States, we saw the importance of staying out of foreign wars. During Washington's presidency the British and French were having another war. The Americans were allies with France, and the British were attempting to provoke America into a war by convincing the Native Americans to attack settlers in the West. Engaging in a war with the Natives as well as the British would have placed the U.S. in a dire situation. Washington realized that fighting a war is expensive. The costs would not have been with just the funds needed to properly fund the war. Losing trade options would have been another cost to the young country. Even though the United States is much more as a union and economically than what we were in Washington's day, this concept of non-interventionism still applies to us today.

As a veteran of the Afghan and Iraq Wars, it took awhile for me to adopt this non-interventionist foreign policy. The stated missions of these wars were to establish a democracy for the respective peoples. This was a noble cause. Two groups of people were allowed for the first time in their lives to engage in the democratic process of voting. Al-Qaeda, the Taliban, and other terrorists groups threatened to attack the voting precincts if people showed up. The people showed up and took part in the democratic process. The only thing left to do was to keep the two countries secure long enough to phase the responsibility of keeping the nations secure over to their respective militaries. Due to political whims here in the United States, this did not happen. We left Afghanistan and Iraq with no regards to what may become of these two struggling nations. Trillions of dollars spent and thousands of lives lost on nothing more than a political whim. In a few years that region will be even more unstable than what it was when we invaded. Much work will have to be done to get back to the level of success that we were at when we left. I cannot justify sending my children off to fight another country's war when I have seen first hand that the politicians in Washington place absolutely no value on the lives or efforts of American service members. If I cannot justify sending my children over there to fight, then I cannot justify sending your children over there to fight either.

What about ISIS? What about it? Anytime that there is a boogey man over there the media and politicians act like we need to send someone else (meaning someone other than the person calling for war) over there to do something about it. It is time to accept the fact that our involvement in other countries' affairs have unintended consequences. ISIS is one of these unintended consequences. ISIS can only exist in a world that has an unstable Iraq. If Saddam Hussein were still in power, he would have crushed ISIS the moment that they began their first operation. Was Saddam Hussein a bad character? Of course he was. Was that a legitimate reason to invade his country and topple his regime? In hindsight we realize that the U.S. government does not value the dollars or lives cost to attempt such a feat. Having the U.S. government engage in military operations with absolutely no thought to the cost in dollars or lives or whether or not the mission will actually be accomplished is a rather frightening position to support.

We needed to get revenge on Osama bin Laden

and Al-Qaeda! Absolutely. Their unprovoked attacks on the United States on 9/11 were not justified. They claimed that we had no business conducting military operations from a country when the King of that country authorized us to do so. (I'm not saying that we were justified in carrying out Operation Southern Watch) Osama bin Laden along with a large number of people believe that their religious views should have more of an influence than the sovereignties of the Middle East. There are some sovereignties that provided support to bin Laden and those that supported his cause. The U.S. killed bin Laden in Pakistan just a few blocks from the Pakistani equivalent to West Point. For years bin Laden had been living in a luxurious compound in Pakistan, obviously at the expense of the Pakistani government. This isn't the only time that the Pakistani government aided bin Laden and Al-Qaeda. During the Afghan war, the Taliban and Al-Qaeda were allowed to cross over into Pakistan at one point on the border, travel through Pakistan then re-enter Afghanistan through another border crossing. During this entire time of playing cat and mouse at the border, the United States was providing aid to Pakistan. What sense does it make to provide aid to a country that is going to aid our enemy while we are at war?

Saddam Hussein was a dangerous man and had to go! If that was the case, why was it the responsibility of the United States to remove him from power? The nations of the Middle East are some of the wealthiest nations on the planet. They can afford to provide for their own defense. If Iraq was such a threat to the region then the Shiites, Sunnis, Israelis, Kurds, and Turks could put aside their differences long enough to deal with this threat. They could have developed a plan for a post war region with no Iraq. But there was no need to do something such as this. The United States has acted as the puppet for the Saudi government for some time now. Until we either get an "America first" type president, or the People of the United States quit wanting to spend dollars and lives over there this will not change. Furthermore, Saddam Hussein would have never been a threat to the region if he were not backed by the United States during the Iraq-Iran War. The U.S. provided billions in loans to Hussein so he could afford to fight a multi-year war with Iran. After the war Iraq was billions in debt and this led to the invasion of Kuwait. Even though relations with Iran were somewhat challenging in the early 80s, freeing the American hostages could have been accomplished in a more reasonable way than arming a dictator.

Looking back at the major conflicts that the United

States has been involved in for the past few decades gives the impression that very little thought is put into whether or not we should intervene with our military. Even less thought is put into the value of the money spent or the number of lives that will be loss. Many of the problems that we have faced could have been avoided if diplomacy would have been engaged. Once you realize that spending trillions of dollars on other country's wars and losing the lives of our service members is not the best course of action, then adopting a non-interventionist foreign policy is easier to embrace.

Abortion

This is an issue that libertarians do not agree on. We will probably not change each other's mind on the issue. I know many pro-life libertarians as well as many pro-choice libertarians. Each side has people that feel strongly about the issue. The discussion often becomes heated because people feel so passionate about the issue. There are also people that do not feel strongly about the issue. Many people are not willing to discuss the merits of the issue. Libertarian philosophy would have to ask, is this even an appropriate issue for the government to address?

In the Libertarian Party's Platform 1.5, it addressed the Party's stance on the issue. It simply states, "We believe that the government should be kept out of the matter." This is not to say that we approve or disapprove of abortion.

If you feel that this is an appropriate role for the government, please reflect back to the "there ought to be a law" section. If a woman decides to have an abortion, should she go to jail? Should paramilitary personnel shoot her?

Reflecting back to the "Classical Liberal" section, we see a glimpse of how government grows and under which circumstances that growth is justified. Taking this approach to the growth of government, is there justification for the government to step into someone's life and make a decision such as this?

If the government does not address abortion, does this mean that we allow it to happen? That is hardly the case. There is tendency that the only way to address an issue is to use the law. This is a perversion of the law. The law is not there to send armed paramilitary personnel throughout the land enforcing whatever our will happens to be at the given time.

Stopping the growth of government and reducing the size of government means that there will be issues that the government will no longer be involved in. Sure, this is a sensitive issue. For many people it is their top issue. If this happens to be your top issue and you come to the public square and say that you would like to have armed paramilitary personnel enforce your will on the rest of us, regardless of what your position is, then we have a conflict. For many of us, we do not need government for this issue. Bringing government to the table for this issue is grounds for leaving the table. What I mean by this is that I do not need the government to ensure that I am pro life. Government should only be involved in the necessities.

Is it necessary to defend the unborn child? Sure it is, to a degree. If a woman is attacked and harm is caused to her child then a crime has been committed. Should a woman be forced to give birth to the child of the man that raped her? If so, instead of sending armed paramilitary personnel to force your will on her you should go do it yourself. If you are not willing to pick up a gun and enforce a decision yourself, then you should not send someone else to do it for you.

Is abortion ending a life? Of course it is. We all know this. But what many people do not realize is that the pro-choice movement came from the eugenics movement of the 1930s. The idea was to get rid of the undesirables in society. The undesirables were considered the poor, uneducated, mentally ill, and unmoral peoples. The elites that supported the pro-choice movement believed that society would be better off without these people. They still believe this. There is no dispute that those who would end the life of their child for no other purpose than not wanting to be a parent is an immoral purpose. The only question is how should you convince them to act somewhat morally; by putting a barrel of a gun in their face or by using grace and care?

Let's consider for a moment that the Republican party has consistently been the "Pro-Life" party, and the Party of self-proclaimed "Conservatives", and a majority (if not all in the last 30 years) have been staunchly "Pro-Life." Consider for a moment these dates: Jan 3, 2001, to Jan 3, 2007. What happened during those dates? For 2 terms under George W. Bush, the House, the Senate, and the Presidency were all Republican Controlled. This was the first time since the passage of Roe vs. Wade in 1973, that both houses AND the White House were controlled by the "Pro-Life Party". The Pro-Life, Republican Party could have easily passed any number of legislation to overturn Roe V Wade, especially since from 2003 - 2007 they had enough members of Congress in both houses that they didn't need to try and get a Democrat to support it. So why didn't they?

Simple: POLITICS. By keeping the Abortion debate, which is always a highly contested debate between the R's and the D's, alive, they are securing voting blocs. Nothing more, nothing less, pure politics. The Republicans DO NOT CARE about Abortion, because if they did, they would have done something about it. There is one man who stood up to do something about it.

In 2005, in the 109th Congress (as well as 110, 111, and 112), Ron Paul (R-TX) re-introduced the Sanctity of Life Bill. This was a bill first introduced in 1995, when Republicans controlled both houses during Bill Clinton's presidency and as expected, failed. So, why is it, that both the Sanctity of

Life bill and the We The People bill (meant to keep private decisions including reproduction, out of government and the justice system's control) never made it through Congress? POLITICS! The most libertarian leaning (and former Libertarian Presidential candidate) proposes a bill that most, if not all pro-lifers would support doesn't get traction in Congress, but every other single Representative for the Republican party ran on a "Pro-Life" ticket, but failed to support Paul's bill. This only proves that the Republican party has no interest in overturning Roe v Wade.

PART IV
Government and the Marketplace

Education or Indoctrination

Election year is always the same. A politician seeks office or reelection. They talk about their plans for your life. One aspect of their plan usually involves education. If the politician is seeking state office then the campaign talk revolves around stronger schools, taking the schools back from Washington, and convincing Washington to just hand money over to fund the schools. If the politician is in a federal office, then there are promises of raising standards again (even though the already-high standards are not what constitutes the problem with the schools) and promising to gain more funding for the state schools while not mentioning any type of needless and overburdensome strings that will come attached to the funding. Is this needed? The way that the system currently works, is this necessary? Should the government, at the federal or state level, be in control of education? Does the government have a vested interest in education? Is this system needed? Is this the best that can be done?

Does the state have a vested interest in education? Yes, the state does have a vested interest in education. The state needs an educated populace to ensure the survival of the state. The state also needs an educated populace to ensure the prosperity of the state. In order for there to be a stable balanced society, there must be an educated populace. Whether it is defense experts, promoting the sciences, or whatever the field is, an educated populace is required for the sake of manning the various fields. It should go without saying that in a liberty-based conversation the government would not pick which fields that these people go into. The people can choose that for themselves based on criteria that they thought should be used.

Should government be in control of education? Well, if they are in control of education then they have the authority to choose what the curriculum will be as well as will not be.

If this is what is meant by government control of education, that every student must be enrolled in a government approved curriculum then the answer would be no. The government should not have a monopoly over education. The government should not hold a monopoly over the authority to educate or a monopoly over the development of curriculum.

A parent should be able to choose which education path is best for the child. Whether it be homeschool, co-opt, private school, charter school, or public school this is a choice for the parent to make in the best interest of the child with no undue influence from the government or local school district. Undue influence must be mentioned because far too often school administrators, the teacher unions, and others in the public education industry stand in the way of what may be best for the student for no other reason than preservation of a system that does not work for every student. This is not to say that there are not benefits to the public education system, because there are. This is, instead, simply saying that the fact that those that profit from the public school industry will hinder what is in the best interest of a student for no other reason than self-preservation. This alone is reason that the government and its subsidiaries cannot have a monopoly over the authority to educate.

When a parent or guardian decides that the public school system is not in the best interest of the child, the student must not be bound to the curriculum of the public school system. Curriculum is a factor for some parents when withdrawing the student from public school. The public school system has a one-size fits all approach to education. In the high school years there are advanced courses. But this approach taken by the public school system causes many subjects to be neglected. This is not necessarily good or bad. It is just the nature of a system that is responsible for educating so many students. When you group 20-30 students into a classroom together, flexibility seems to be sacrificed. If the central planners would allow the local school boards to have control of the curriculum, then subjects such as financial education, critical thinking, etc. could have a place in the public schools. The local school board guiding the process of adopting curriculum and courses would be more proper than the strings being pulled by a central bureaucracy that is not familiar with the student body.

Currently central planners manage the public school system. Each state has a Board of Education that adopts standards and curriculum. Each state has its own requirements to be on the Board of Education. A lot of work is continually put into a new system. But is a new system constantly needed? If its educational material is staying the same for the most part, then all that is needed is a particular standard to meet a particular goal. If there is going to be a state Board of Education then instead of dictating policy, the Board of Education should communicate with the universities and colleges in that state. The primary purpose of this communication should be to determine which standard of education and competency is needed to enroll and be successful at that particular institution. Once these standards are developed, then the state Board of Education should assist local school boards in developing and adapting curriculum to help the students obtain the particular standard of education and competency that meets the student's goals. This would allow the educator to actually educate without the bureaucrats getting in the way.

If Washington cannot dictate the terms of education, should Washington be involved at all? In an ideal situation Washington would not be involved in education and neither would the state governments. But we are dealing with a less than ideal situation. How do we improve the system from here? If we keep the current system of funding the government, that is to say that we still have massive revenue and the federal government has a balanced budget with revenue set aside for education, how should Washington be involved? We have already determined that Washington has no place setting curriculum standards or pushing its agenda on the school system. Is there anything left that Washington can do? Improving facilities would be a good role for Washington. Many school districts are poor, which means that they are underfunded. Buildings fall into dilapidation and need improvements or complete replacement. If Washington wants a role, then this might be the best role for Washington to take. If Washington did supply funding for this, would it be possible for Washington to leave the rest of education up to those who are best at educating? Or would Washington feel the need to once again attach strings to the funds?

The public school system receives funding from three primary sources: the locality in which it is located via property taxes, the state government, and the federal government. If someone owns a home, then the state and local government taxes this ownership. In other words, if you do not pay the tax that comes with owning property then the property may be confiscated through current legal processes. People often overlook this discrepancy in the understanding of liberty because there is a direct reward in paying the tax. The reward is the public school system. Even if people do not have school aged children, they typically do not mind paying the school tax because they went to public school. For the people that own homes and decided that the public school system was not the best choice for their child, these people have to pay twice. They pay the property tax to fund the public school. Then they have to pay the price to either home school or private school the child. It is not right to force a parent to pay for an institution when a parent had to seek an education for the child elsewhere.

There are two ways to remedy the situation. The first way would be to reduce, or eliminate the school taxes of a parent of a school-aged child. This would not cover the entire cost of the private education, but it would greatly contribute. The second choice would be to allow the parent & student to choose which programs that the child would like to use. If a homeschooling child would like to take part in extra-curricular activities, such as sports, band, drama, or any particular academic class, it should be acceptable for the student to come in for that class or program then return to the home or private school. If the parent must fund the public school system, then the parent should be able to pick which classes or programs could supplement the private education.

Like many issues we see the politicians work the public during campaign season. And the public gets worked up. The conversation quickly turns into political propaganda and the people become sharply divided over an issue that should not be divisive at all. You will never see a politician suggest handing education over to those who are educated in the various subjects. You will not see this because it does not build momentum for the political machine. For some reason people are more likely to turn out to vote when they are upset or promised something. Education is one of the tools that the politicians use to get votes. With that being said, it is time to realize that education is too important to leave in the hands of the political class. There should be a wall built between education and state.

Healthcare and the Free Market

"So this is where you are going to tell me how I should be ashamed because I'm on Medicare?"

No, this isn't meant to make anyone feel bad, but rather to show how a change in the perception of government can actually lead to common sense solutions that would be easy to implement. Besides, if you do receive Medicare, (A) you paid into that system all your working life, and (B) you have bigger issues to worry about.

With the passage of the Affordable Care Act (AKA Obamacare), many people thought that they would be getting free healthcare. Many Socialists celebrated thinking that their Dear Leader was going to take care of them and stick it to the big insurance carriers. Ironically, the big insurance providers just got subsidized by the government and a plethora of forced customers. However, the problem with our healthcare system is not Obamacare or the health insurance companies, or even the health care providers themselves. The real issue is that the government both regulates the healthcare industry as well as participates in the industry. This presents the basic "conflict of interest" situation that people generally attempt to steer clear of. However, in America, it is embraced.

When the government regulates and participates in the healthcare industry, the problem is similar to playing a game where the best player makes up the rules as they go and they can do things that you aren't allowed to do. But let's dive into some real examples so that you fully understand the problem.

Medicare/Medicaid reimburses doctors 60-70% of the billable services and it reimburses Hospitals 30-40% of billable services. What this means is that the same bill that they send to a cash payer (who is responsible for 100% of the bill) the government basically says, "No, you'll take what we give you." But how does this increase the costs of health care?

EXAMPLE #1

A family doctor's total costs per hour breaks down to $30. This is the bare minimum that he needs to keep the bills paid, the lights on, and the staff paid. This does NOT include his income. He charges $40 for an office visit. Meaning that the business makes a profit of $10 per hour (provided it takes at least 1 hour per patient and he only sees 1 patient at a time). So, let's put this into a table and compare Medicare/Medicaid, Private insurance, and Cash only:

	Cash Only	Insurance	Medicare/caid
Office Visit Price	$40	$40	$40
% Paid by Entity	100%	80%	60%
$Paid by Entity	$40	$32	$24
$ Paid by Patient	$40	$20 co-pay	$0
Profit	$10	$52	$-16

So, the doctor will take a $16 LOSS for every Medicare/medicaid patient that he sees. And when you consider that about 80% of most doctor's patients are Medicare/Medicaid, that could be a significant loss. If he sees 200 patients in 1 week, at 80% Medicare patients, the total loss from Medicare/caid patients would total $2,560. Even if the remaining 20% were Insurance patients, the net loss would be $480 per week. NO BUSINESS can stay open operating at a loss of $500 per month.

What is the doctor to do? Simply, increase the price of the office visit. So he increases it by 50% from $40, to $60. Let's take a look at that table:

	Cash Only	Insurance	Medicare/caid
Office Visit Price	$60	$60	$60
% Paid by Entity	100%	80%	60%

$Paid by Entity	$0	$48	$36
$ Paid by Patient	$60	$20 co-pay	$0
Profit	$30	$8	$6

So, now he's turning a profit, but not much of one. He's only getting $6 per office visit from the Medicare/caid patient. I believe, if my calculations are correct $6.00/hour is less than $7.25/hour which is below national minimum wage.

Yes, these numbers are "for example", but you can see that in order to turn a profit, if only for survival of the business, a doctor's office can cause an increase in health care costs. But the more drastic increase to health care costs comes at the hospitals.

EXAMPLE 2

You break your arm on Saturday when your doctor's office is not open, and you have to go to your local hospital's emergency room. You stay there for 2 hours getting X-rays and casting of your arm. The actual cost of said services (including labor, materials, and overhead) is $750. Let's take a look at what would happen if the hospital needed to make a minimum of 10% profit on all patients, what that would look like.

	Cash Only	Insurance	Medicare/caid

ER Visit Price	$825	$825	$825
% Paid by Entity	100%	80%	40%
$Paid by Entity	$0	$660	$330
$ Paid by Patient	$825	$165	$0
Profit	$75	$165	$-495

For every Medicare/medicaid patient that is seen by a hospital emergency room, they need to see 3 insurance patients or 7 cash only patients. The problem is that most of the cash only patients will most likely not pay in a timely fashion, if at all. So, let's take a look at what it would take for the hospital to make money on all patients.

Since Medicare/caid is going to be paying less than ½ of the billable services, we need to increase by 100% + difference between percentage paid by medicare/caid. Keeping in mind that the hospital would still like to make 10% profit on all patients, this would mean the minimum billed would for $750 in services would have to be $2,145.

	Cash Only	Insurance	Medicare/caid

ER Visit Price	$2,145	$2,145	$2,145
% Paid by Entity	100%	80%	40%
$Paid by Entity	$0	$1,716	$858
$ Paid by Patient	$2,145	$429	$0
Profit	$1,395	$165	$108

These examples include some assumptions, mainly that your insurance deductible is reached and you have an 80/20 split after deductible. Otherwise, the best that will happen is an insurance re-price which will reduce the amount you pay, but it will be more like the amount that would otherwise be paid by the insurance company.

"Why doesn't the hospital or the doctor's office just offer different prices based on how the customer is going to pay?"

That would be a WONDERFUL idea, and it makes sense. But it is against the regulations laid forth by Medicare and Medicaid and it binds the doctors offices and hospitals from offering drastically different prices for services paid by the government and services paid by the people. If you notice, also, that between the two tables, the private insurance company now has to pay 260% more than before, this means that payout affects their bottom line. When something affects the bottom line, things have to change, and unlike retail items, the hassle of buying new healthcare and starting over with another company allows the insurance providers the comfort in knowing that their customers won't leave so easily, and now, under Obamacare, they run a risk of getting fined for any time they did not have adequate coverage. This enables the insurance companies the easy of sliding their monthly premiums up sometimes 10-20% year after year. Because, after all, they merely have to send out a well written, empathetic letter explaining that they don't like increasing rates, but it is necessary due to the increasing healthcare costs. Because of this regulation, as well as Government participation in Healthcare, it is easy to see how the natural move for insurance companies would be to increase premiums to make up for the increased cost caused by the losses because of Medicare/Medicaid.

One solution to the insurance issue, even with government participation, would be to break down the barriers that prevent a person in Mississippi from purchasing a Vermont insurance policy. Especially when you consider that some of the big insurance companies operate in multiple (if not all) the states, and therefore would be able to easily craft insurance policies that could meet any state minimum requirements (were there any.) But this doesn't fall solely on the shoulders of the federal government, but also rests in control of the State Insurance Commissioner.

Retirement

There are many different types of retirement accounts that a person may have. Some of them are taxable. Clearly there is nothing that is off limits to the regime in Washington. The Congress believes that it has the moral authority to plunder any form of income that a person has at any time that they would like. Even the beloved Social Security is subject to these raids. The Congress has proven that it does not respect property rights in regards to income. This lack of regard for the sanctity of retirement funds coupled with the fact that one should not be bound to the financial advice of the Congress is why retirement should be completely left alone by the government.

Even though retirement income is still income, it will be addressed as a separate issue in this conversation. As long as income is taxable, all retirement income should be tax exempt. By tax exempt I mean that the money contributed to the retirement fund should not be taxable. When the money comes out of the retirement fund during retirement, it should not be taxed at all. This includes all retirement accounts whether they be pensions, 401(k), individual retirement account, etc. If an account is marked for retirement and money is drawn from those accounts during the retirement years, then there should not be any taxes associated with it. After a lifetime of paying income tax, the person should get a break. It should also be noted that many people have a lower income while living during retirement. This is also a reason not to tax retirement.

Social Security is a pyramid. It is a Ponzi scheme. I am not saying that there is no benefit. There is a benefit. Many people have depended on this program in the past. Many use it now. Some will be using it in the near future. Unfortunately with the way the system was designed, it will eventually collapse due to too many recipients withdrawing money. This is not their fault. They paid into the system. They are owed a retirement. That can never be argued. The only argument or discussion that can take place is how long will we allow the Congress to keep people trapped in a system that will collapse?

For years Congress has battled over whether or not to try and fix Social Security. The only years that they did not argue over this were when they were raiding the Social Security fund to acquire extra revenue for the budget. Social Security is an important issue for many Americans but Congress has no plans to fix it. The only use that they get out of the program is to use it to pit American citizens against each other during election year. This is an abuse of power and it needs to end. Retirement is too important of an issue to use it as a political talking point during election year. It is time to take this abusive power away from Congress and privatize retirement.

Privatizing retirement frightens some people because they think that they will lose their retirement. This would not be the case if we transitioned away from Social Security. Those that are currently on Social Security as well as those that are up to an undetermined amount of time away from retirement should be allowed to stay with Social Security. Those entering the workforce up to those that are up to an undetermined amount of time away from retirement would have to use private funds for retirement.

There are some unknowns in the equation. Understandably that will make some people uncomfortable. But this is a problem that has to be addressed. As people begin to leave the Social Security program for private retirement, they cannot be expected to contribute to the Social Security program anymore. This would not be right. Forcing people to continue to contribute to this failed program would just cause people to be entrapped in it. This revenue has to come from somewhere else. Other programs will have to be eliminated.

LIBERTARIANISM IN A NUTSHELL

Welfare

Welfare was the centerpiece of the Great Society program ushered in by President Lyndon B Johnson. It was supposed to lift people out of poverty. It was supposed to be a safety net that would help families struggle through the tough times. The "Great Charity" as some believe it to be. While it has provided some good, it replaced private charity and grew the lower class. It's time to open this discussion back up and reconsider if we should have it.

It seems that a disclaimer should always be mentioned when a conversation about welfare begins. Yes, I care about poor people. Yes, I want them to have help. No, I do not think that they are gaming the system. A few might, but most of them are not. I can comfortably say this because only a few people are caught gaming the system. If there is a study or report that says otherwise, please present it and we will discuss it.

In the conversation concerning welfare, no one ever mentions the number of families that are generational users of welfare. When I use this term "generational users" I am not referring to the welfare queen and her eight children. I am not referring to families that game the system to have another source of income. I am referring to the people that end up depending on the welfare program because their parents did not teach them any better. How many 2nd, 3rd, etc generational users of the program exist? Does this information exist? If not, then why not? If this is a generational issue, as many believe it is, why would the government not want to identify it as an issue and seek to remedy the situation? Why would the government now want to help the lower class climb up the ladder? The reason is because the government does not care if the lower class climbs up the ladder of success. If the government can provide a little bit of benefits, people will keep voting for them. Even the lower middle class will buy into this. If people were financially educated, they would have a better chance of climbing up the ladder of success.

Politicians like to keep certain key issues at hand to keep the base worked up. Welfare happens to be one that the Left likes to use. Hans Sennholz discusses this in his book "The Politics of Unemployment." If Congress created an environment that allowed business to prosper instead of burdening them with undue regulations, then more people would be able to find work. But they don't do this. They create an environment that causes much unemployment. This unemployment and the potential for unemployment is the bait that the politicians use to trick the electorate during the campaign. It's rather sad that American politics revolves around such trickery. If the smoke and mirrors tactic was not used, then Congress would have to focus on their actual job instead of bribing voters.

Part V
Applying the Principles of Liberty

The easiest ways to apply the principles of liberty is not to solve problems caused by the government with more government, but rather to keep in mind this simple quote from Thomas Jefferson, "it does me no harm if my neighbor says there are twenty gods, or no God; whatever does not pick my pocket or break my leg." Simply put, people are entitled to nothing but their own opinions, no matter how flawed you may think those might be, those are their opinions and only experience to the contrary will change their views.

First and foremost, you will not win anyone to libertarianism by beating them over the head with the writings of Milton Friedman or Murray Rothbard, no more than you will win someone to Christ by beating them in the head with a Bible. There are a few main points that you MUST remember in order to apply the principles of liberty:

1.   All laws are enforced at the barrel of a gun. So remember before you cry out "There ought to be a law" remember, you are advocating for someone to physically harm another because you think a law should be in place.

2.   Theft is the forceful taking of another's property. Slavery is the forceful taking of another's labor. If you advocate for more

taxation, you are not only advocating theft, but slavery in part, because in order for there to be theft of personal property, there must be labor first to produce it.

3.   Liberty is a double-edged sword. What you advocate for can also be used against you. Right now (in 2016) there's a lot of talk about "Religious Freedom Bills" that merely enforce the long understood "Right to Refuse" by enabling people with religious or moral obligations to opt out of participating in something they do not agree with. Primarily this is used to protect religious people from being legally sued by people who cry "discrimination" because someone doesn't agree with your gay marriage. However, remember...double-edged sword. A gay baker can also refuse to make a wedding cake for someone who opposes gay marriage.

What it all really boils down to is this: Respect everyone. You don't have to agree with their philosophy, their religion, their lifestyle, their choices to be able to just get along with them. If you find yourself in a debate where it is causing you to lose your cool, step away. Your points won't matter anymore and it appears that winning is the only thing that becomes important. Understand that not everyone will agree with you, but learn to live with that being okay. It takes us all to make the world go around. Life is more important than losing a friend over their support of Trump or Clinton or Sanders or Cruz...or McAfee or Petersen.

Understand that in order for America to survive, things have to change. When you consider that since the election of Abraham Lincoln in 1861, the political landscape has been Republicans vs Democrats. We have done it their way, and look where it has gotten America: $20 TRILLION in debt, failing social programs, unchecked collusion between large corporations and life-long politicians. I will quote Ronald Reagan again, not because he was a good president (trust me, he made significant failures), but he understood the principles of liberty. Reagan said, "Government is not the solution to the problem. Government IS the problem."

Appendices

Appendix A: Recommended Reading

- <u>The Law</u> by Frederic Bastiat

- <u>Defending the Undefendable</u> by Walter Block

- <u>Income Tax: The Root of All Evil</u> by Frank Chodorov

- <u>The Road to Serfdom</u> by F.A. Hayek

- <u>Economics in One Lesson</u> by Henry Hazlitt

- <u>Deflation and Liberty</u> by Jorg Guido Hulsmann

- <u>Human Action</u> by Ludwig von Mises

- <u>Liberty and Property</u> by Ludwig von Mises

- <u>End the Fed</u> by Ron Paul

- <u>The Revolution: A Manifesto</u> by Ron Paul

- <u>A Foreign Policy of Freedom</u> by Ron Paul

- <u>The Case for a 100 Percent Gold Dollar</u> by Murray Rothbard

- <u>The Case Against the Fed</u> by Murray Rothbard

- <u>Education: Free and Compulsory</u> by Murray Rothbard

LIBERTARIANISM IN A NUTSHELL

Appendix B: Bibliography

- Bastiat, Frederic. *The Law*. France (1850). E-book/PDF

- Goldman, Emma. *Anarchism and Other Essays*. Mineola, NY: Dover Publications. Print

- Rothbard, Murray. *Man, Economy and State, with Power and Market – Scholar's Edition*. Auburn, AL: Ludwig von Mises Institute. Print

  - Wolff, Robert Paul. *In Defense of Anarchism*. Berkley: University of California Press. Print

Made in United States
North Haven, CT
16 October 2022